Legal Problems of International Organizations

Felice Morgenstern was one of the leading international organizations lawyers of her generation, producing first-rate academic work based on her vast practical experience, gained as a legal official at the International Labour Organization. This reissue of her classic Lauterpacht lectures delivered at Cambridge University in 1985 (with a Foreword by Jan Klabbers) discusses three issues in the law of international organizations: their position in public and private international law; issues of membership and representation; and standard-setting. Long out of stock, this reissue makes Morgenstern's pioneering work available to a new generation of students of international organizations law.

FELICE MORGENSTERN (1926–2000) was educated at Cambridge University, was the first female Whewell scholar at Cambridge (in 1948), and subsequently spent some three decades as a legal officer with the International Labour Organization in Geneva.

JAN KLABBERS is Professor of International Law at the University of Helsinki. He is the author of a number of articles on international organizations law, authored *An Introduction to International Organizations Law* (4th edn, Cambridge University Press, 2022), and edited *The Cambridge Companion to International Organizations Law* (Cambridge University Press, 2022).

Recent books in the Hersch Lauterpacht Memorial Lecture Series

Michael Wood and Eran Sthoeger *The UN Security Council and International Law*

Tom Ginsburg *Democracies and International Law*

Christine Chinkin *Women, Peace and Security and International Law*

Stephen M. Schwebel, Luke Sobota and Ryan Manton *International Arbitration: Three Salient Problems*

Mary Ellen O'Connell *The Art of Law in the International Community*

Yuval Shany *Questions of Jurisdiction and Admissibility before International Courts*

W. Michael Reisman and Christina Skinner *Fraudulent Evidence before Public International Tribunals: The Dirty Stories of International Law*

Andrés Rigo Sureda *Investment Treaty Arbitration: Judging under Uncertainty*

Ralph Zacklin *The United Nations Secretariat and the Use of Force in a Unipolar World: Power v. Principle*

John H. Jackson *Sovereignty, the WTO, and Changing Fundamentals of International Law*

Jan Paulsson *Denial of Justice in International Law*

Francisco Orrego Vicuña *International Dispute Settlement in an Evolving Global Society: Constitutionalization, Accessibility, Privatization*

Martti Koskenniemi *The Gentle Civilizer of Nations: The Rise and Fall of International Law 1870–1960*

Thomas M. Franck *Recourse to Force: State Action against Threats and Armed Attacks*

Mohamed Shahabuddeen *Precedent in the World Court*

Antonio Cassese *Self-Determination of Peoples: A Legal Reappraisal*

Legal Problems of International Organizations

Reissue with New Foreword by Jan Klabbers

FELICE MORGENSTERN
University of Helsinki

CAMBRIDGE
UNIVERSITY PRESS

CAMBRIDGE
UNIVERSITY PRESS

Shaftesbury Road, Cambridge CB2 8EA, United Kingdom

One Liberty Plaza, 20th Floor, New York, NY 10006, USA

477 Williamstown Road, Port Melbourne, VIC 3207, Australia

314–321, 3rd Floor, Plot 3, Splendor Forum, Jasola District Centre,
New Delhi – 110025, India

103 Penang Road, #05–06/07, Visioncrest Commercial, Singapore 238467

Cambridge University Press is part of Cambridge University Press & Assessment,
a department of the University of Cambridge.

We share the University's mission to contribute to society through the pursuit of
education, learning and research at the highest international levels of excellence.

www.cambridge.org
Information on this title: www.cambridge.org/9781009448185

DOI: 10.1017/9781009448154

Grotius Publications Limited 1986

Reissue Cambridge University Press & Assessment 2024

A catalogue record for this publication is available from the British Library

Library of Congress Cataloging-in-Publication Data
Names: Morgenstern, Felice, author. | Klabbers, Jan, writer of foreword.
Title: Legal problems of international organizations : reissue with new foreword by Jan
Klabbers / Felice Morgenstern ; Jan Klabbers, University of Helsinki.
Description: Cambridge, United Kingdom ; New York, NY : Cambridge University Press,
2023. | Series: Ghlm hersch lauterpacht memorial lectures | Includes bibliographical
references and index.
Identifiers: LCCN 2023031979 (print) | LCCN 2023031980 (ebook) |
ISBN 9781009448185 (hardback) | ISBN 9781009448147 (paperback) |
ISBN 9781009448154 (epub)
Subjects: LCSH: International agencies–Law and legislation.
Classification: LCC KZ4850 .M657 2023 (print) | LCC KZ4850 (ebook)
LC record available at https://lccn.loc.gov/2023031979
LC ebook record available at https://lccn.loc.gov/2023031980

ISBN 978-1-009-44818-5 Hardback

Contents

Foreword

Jan Klabbers[1]

A. Introduction

It has been nearly four decades since Felice Morgenstern delivered her 'Lauterpacht lectures' and published them in book form as *Legal Problems of International Organizations*. The book serves as something of an informal litmus test for international organization lawyers: one of those classic texts that one simply must have read at some point. Why some books acquire this status and others do not remains mysterious, something sociologists of science may wish to investigate in order to come to a general hypothesis, but in Morgenstern's case the answer seems fairly straightforward, and consists of two, maybe three, elements.

The first element resides in the circumstance that Morgenstern combined academic acumen and practical experience in a highly felicitous manner, and had done so throughout her career. While her work is recognizably doctrinal–academic in the best Cambridge tradition, the questions she asks herself are invariably inspired by practical issues: much of her work is characterized by her spotting a practical question, giving rise to academic reflection. A typical example is her classic article on how the law of the international civil service conceptualizes the notion of 'family', a notion of some relevance in that dependants of officials can be entitled to benefits — it seems more than likely that the question was inspired by her experiences as a lawyer working for the International Labour Organization (I.L.O.).[2] She may have encountered the question posed

[1] Professor of International Law, University of Helsinki. I am indebted to Sarah Nouwen for her help in retrieving some materials. This Foreword forms part of the PRIVIGO project funded by the European Research Council, Grant number 883417.

[2] Felice Morgenstern, "The Law Applicable to International Officials" (1969) 18 *I.C.L.Q.*, 739-56.

by others in her daily work, and may have been wondering about it from her own position, as an unmarried woman with a live-in mother. Either way, while the resulting article is of high academic quality, there is nothing 'academic' about the question. Often, with Morgenstern, the academic and the practical form a balanced combination.

A second reason why *Legal Problems* has become one of those classics is that it is one of the first more or less general texts on international organizations written by a woman. That is not to say women had not been writing about international organizations law before. Suzanne Bastid (née Basdevant) wrote a path-breaking monograph on the law of the international civil service in the early 1930s.[3] Ingrid Detter wrote an insightful book on law-making by international organizations in the mid-1960s,[4] shortly after Rosalyn Higgins had published her classic study on the legal role of the political organs of the United Nations.[5] But all of these were limited to either a single aspect of international organizations law (law-making, civil service law) or a single organization (the U.N.), and much the same applies to studies published around the same time as *Legal Problems*, such as Neri Sybesma-Knol's book on the legal position of observers in the U.N.[6] By contrast, Morgenstern draws on a wealth of materials from a variety of international organizations, and discusses a number of general issues in *Legal Problems*, so much so that the work suggests a more general approach to — and understanding of — international organizations. By discussing different topics within the pages of a single volume and drawing on a diversity of source materials, a deeper insight is hinted at than is usually the case with single-issue monographs.

Third, and much more prosaically, it is not impossible that *Legal Problems* owes some of its reputation to having been unavailable for a while: scarcity may drive up a reputation. The good legal library will have acquired a copy when it first came out, but for those unfortunate enough not to be near such a library, *Legal Problems* has proved hard to locate. Even online, no copies were to be found for a considerable length of time. *Legal Problems*, it turned out, has been out of print for many years, and it is likely that this unavailability has contributed to its status as something of a cult classic. Ironically then, the current reissue may come to undermine its cult status to some extent, but still, on balance, it will be worth it. *Legal Problems*

3 Suzanne Basdevant, *Les fonctionnaires internationaux* (Paris: Sirey, 1931).
4 Ingrid Detter, *Law Making by International Organizations* (Stockholm: Norstedt, 1965).
5 Rosalyn Higgins, *The Development of International Law through the Political Organs of the United Nations* (Oxford University Press, 1963).
6 R.G. Sybesma-Knol, *The Status of Observers in the United Nations* (Brussels: Free University, 1981).

is an excellent piece of scholarship, at some points far ahead of its time and hinting at a novel perspective on international organizations, and it would seem irresponsible not to allow new generations of international organization lawyers to acquaint themselves with such a classic text.

B. The Background

The law of international organizations developed in the late nineteenth and early twentieth century, and has remained more or less unchanged since.[7] The core proposition underlying the dominant approach (often referred to as functionalism, but not to be confused with the functionalism prevailing among political scientists) holds that international organizations are set up by states in order to perform a specific function — to do something states are unable or unwilling to do on their own. Those functions are typically envisaged as merely technical and apolitical, benign and hugely desirable, such as regulating global health or global communications, or harmonizing standards. It follows, so the argument goes (often implicitly), that the world will be a better place if the performance or achievement of that function is stimulated.[8] To that end, international organizations can typically claim far-reaching powers, including 'implied powers': such powers as are necessary to help them perform their function, even if not expressly written down in the constituent instrument. Likewise, international organizations can typically claim a broad catalogue of privileges and immunities from national jurisdiction: anything to enable them to function effectively, without interference by state authorities. And controlling them proves difficult — this is left to the member states, and thus not always terribly effective.

The limits of functionalism are well known by now. With some organizations (the E.U., the U.N.), the function is so broad as to be impossible to identify — as a result, almost any activity can be presented as necessary for the organization. It remains unclear why third parties (contractors, officials, non-member states) should facilitate the work of any given organization, especially in the absence of judicial relief. And the explanatory potential of functionalism, moreover, proves limited: it has little to say

[7] See, generally, Jan Klabbers, "The EJIL Foreword: The Transformation of International Organizations Law" (2015) 26 *European Journal of International Law*, 9-82.

[8] There is an unbroken chain in the legal literature covering well over a century of functionalist thought. The chain starts, in book form, with Paul S. Reinsch, *Public International Unions, their Work and Organization: A Study in International Administrative Law* (Boston: Ginn & Co., 1911), and continues to include H.G. Schermers and Niels M. Blokker, *International Institutional Law: Unity within Diversity*, 6th edn (Leiden: Martinus Nijhoff, 2018).

about relations within organizations (with staff, for example, or between organs), and even less about relations with the outside world. Functionalism, and therewith the entire edifice of international organizations law, is premised on the thought that the only relevant legal relationship is the relationship between the organization and its member states — other legal dynamics are systematically ignored, as if the organization and its members find themselves in a vacuum.[9] This was never based on a realistic description of international organizations and their activities — after all, it would be implausible to hold that I.L.O. recommendations are meant to affect Denmark and France as states, but not Danish or French workers or employers.[10] Still, despite not being plausible, the vacuum assumption has proved an enormously powerful topos.

Legal Problems was delivered as a set of lectures in 1985 and published a year later. This functionalist approach proved the backdrop to Morgenstern's lectures, as it was still the dominant approach in 1985 — indeed, it probably still is, in the 2020s. Against this background, the pioneering aspects of Morgenstern's work become visible, for somehow she refused to limit herself to the vacuum assumption. It is clear, from many asides as well as from some of the topics she covers, that she realized there was a world out there outside and beyond the relationship between the organization and its member states. She did not do this systematically, and she did not always carry things through to their logical conclusion, but she deserves credit for being one of the first to move beyond the vacuum assumption. She opened up a new perspective on international organizations law, perhaps somewhat hesitantly and unwittingly at times, and sometimes hidden beneath a layer of what at first sight looks like a classic functionalist approach.

C. The Young Morgenstern

Felice Morgenstern was born on 23 October 1926 in Vienna, and died in 2000. As a young girl, she moved to England with her family, did well at school, and went on to read History at Cambridge University.[11] This too

[9] Jan Klabbers, "Theorising International Organisations", in Anne Orford and Florian Hoffmann (eds.), *The Oxford Handbook of the Theory of International Law* (Oxford University Press, 2016), 618-34.

[10] Jan Klabbers, "An Accidental Revolution: The ILO and the Opening Up of International Law", in Tarja Halonen and Ulla Liukkunen (eds.), *International Labour Organization and Global Social Governance* (Dordrecht: Springer, 2020), 123-40.

[11] For more biographical detail, see Jan Klabbers, "The Timing of Felice Morgenstern", in Immi Tallgren (ed.), *Portraits of Women in International Law: New Names and Forgotten Faces* (Oxford University Press, 2023), 253.

went very well, and prompted her to embark on a legal career. She read law articles at the Council of Legal Education but, more importantly, also became a student of Sir Hersch Lauterpacht — by his own reckoning one of his very best. She wrote her master's thesis on the right of asylum, having it spawn several scholarly articles. This was followed by a doctoral dissertation on the relationship between international law and domestic law, which likewise spawned several scholarly articles. In February 1952, she was appointed as a legal officer at the I.L.O., where she would spend the rest of her career.

Both her master's thesis and doctoral thesis are meticulous examples of doctrinal work at its best, well researched, containing sharp analytical distinctions, and richly illustrated with authoritative materials, whether court decisions or excerpts from diplomatic practice. As with so much scholarly work from those days and in this tradition, in retrospect it is somewhat parochial (the states whose practices matter are invariably the U.K., the U.S.A., France and a few others), but it clearly shows a brilliant legal mind at work. What is more, it shows an adventurous and insightful legal mind at work: few of her contemporaries would have thought of referring to the competing doctrines of dualism and monism, seen to govern relations between international and domestic law, as two different types of 'machinery'.[12] The image is evocative and would be put to good use a few decades later by critical theorists describing legal processes in similar terms — a term such as 'assemblage' seems similarly inspired.

This is something that happened to Morgenstern more often: she frequently launched a term, an idea or a proposition long before it became standard academic practice. This is what she did with the term 'machinery' — conjuring up images of the bureaucratization of legal process, of something that can be analysed as cool structure, devoid of passion or soul. It is unlikely that she herself thought through all possible consequences and associations, but with the benefit of hindsight, the imagery is striking. And, in a different register, so too is the closing sentence of her doctoral study, which refers, long before doing so became fashionable, to "the international rule of law".[13] Again, one senses that she operates mostly on the level of intuition — there is no systematic elaboration of what the international rule of law could possibly entail, other perhaps than the primacy of international law over domestic law. But the term is striking, and she would later — much later — write insightfully and far more systematically about legality in international law, in particular in

[12] Felice Morgenstern, The Primacy of International Law (doctoral thesis, University of Cambridge, 1953), 392.

[13] *Ibid.*, 397.

the law of international organizations. Enlisting the notion of legality in that manner once again was ahead of the curve.

When Morgenstern started her career, there was really no such thing as international organizations law — at least not as a recognized sub-discipline. Monographs and articles had been published since the 1880s, but the first textbook, for example, was still a decade away from publication.[14] It is no surprise then that the few remarks she made on international organizations law were far from consequential, and by and large reflected the *communis opinio* at the time. In her work on asylum, for example, she referred to various refugee organizations invariably as vehicles for inter-state co-operation, although she does so with regret: these organizations are places where states can pool their resources, but are "not able to compel states to take any particular action, such as admitting refugees".[15] And in classical fashion, she explained that, generally, member states "are not prepared to surrender, in favour of international organs, a sufficient quantity of rights and powers to make the action of these at all effective".[16]

Still, the closing pages of her doctoral dissertation suggest that there might be light at the end of the tunnel: of the then brand-new European Community for Coal and Steel she notes that its organs "take the place of municipal organs in the administration of the common market in coal and steel".[17] And, tantalizingly, she held that this would help to improve the 'machinery', suggestive once again of a link between bureaucracy and international law. This is all the more surprising as much of her early work oozes the spirit of international law as classic inter-state law, binding upon states on the inter-state level and usually envisaged as some kind of private law writ large, and thus without any international machinery being involved. It would be far too strong to claim that Morgenstern inaugurated a new approach to international law — if only for the good reason that her doctoral dissertation was never published. But it is considerably more plausible to claim that she had an intuition that international law reached beyond and inside inter-state co-operation.

D. Morgenstern at Work

In 1930, the Permanent Court of International Justice rendered a rarely noticed advisory opinion on whether the Free City of Danzig, created at

[14] This first textbook was, most likely, Derek W. Bowett, *The Law of International Institutions* (London: Stevens and Sons, 1963).
[15] Felice Morgenstern, *The Right of Asylum* (LLM thesis, University of Cambridge, 1949), 132.
[16] *Ibid.*, 136. [17] Morgenstern, *The Primacy of International Law*, 396.

the Versailles peace conference, could join the International Labour Organization.[18] As advisory opinions go, it never became a very prominent example. It is not often mentioned in the textbooks on international organizations law, nor is it often referred to in specialized studies on membership of international organizations.[19] Partly this is, no doubt, because the setting was somewhat esoteric, too specialized to yield generalizable results. After all, how many entities were created as free states? And how many of those have an agreement with their administering power (Poland) in place? And of those, how many would wish to join an international organization joined at the hip to another one (the League of Nations) which would not be of interest to them? Consequently, the advisory opinion received little attention when it came out,[20] and has received little attention since.

Substantively, moreover, it seems that the Court endorsed a position which, by now, has left the harbour. It eventually held that, while Danzig's status as a Free City, as such, would not bar Danzig from membership, the need to consult Poland in matters affecting Danzig's foreign relations created problems. Unless Poland were to agree in advance to consent to all possible contingencies that might occur (which had not happened), this situation would bar Danzig from joining.

The Court's underlying logic was a functionalist one: without Polish consent, Danzig is unlikely to be able to contribute much to the work of the I.L.O., and thus it is best not to admit it. Around the same time, the functionalist logic had also been in use with the League of Nations when it was confronted with Liechtenstein's application for membership of the League. Liechtenstein, not having an army of its own, was unable to contribute fully to the functions of the League, so the argument went. The same logic was now applied to Danzig: Danzig, not fully in control of its own foreign relations, would not be able to contribute to the functions of the I.L.O.

If the advisory opinion has been all but forgotten, it is all the more remarkable that it features in the academic work of Felice Morgenstern, and does so not just once, but twice. Moreover, she makes use of it in two different ways, illustrating different points, and therewith also emphasizing her own intellectual ambivalence. The skilful lawyer can engage in

18 *Free City of Danzig and International Labour Organization, P.C.I.J.* Series B, no. 18 (1930).

19 But see the brief discussion in Alison Duxbury, *The Participation of States in International Organisations* (Cambridge University Press, 2011), 71.

20 It was briefly reported on, though not deeply engaged with, by Alexander Fachiri, "Advisory Opinion No. 18. Delivered August 26, 1930", 12 *B.Y.* 164-6 (1931), and Manly O. Hudson, "The Ninth Year of the Permanent Court of International Justice", 25 *A.J.I.L.* 1-25, 4-8 (1931).

something akin to conceptual pluralism: a rule or a decision may support a particular point one day but, in a different light, support a different point the next day.[21] In a classic article from the mid-1970s, she uses the *Danzig/I.L.O.* opinion to discuss the veritable absence of admission criteria in the I.L.O. Constitution. She notes that the Court hardly discusses the one explicit requirement: I.L.O. membership is only open for members of the League of Nations. P.C.I.J. President Anzilotti had highlighted this in his dissent in 1930, but it was not discussed in any detail by the majority. Yet the same I.L.O. was happy enough in 1934 to admit as one of its members the U.S.A., which, as is well known, never was a member of the League of Nations. Three years later, moreover, it also admitted Egypt without that state being a member of the League. For Morgenstern, the admission of the U.S.A. and later Egypt is difficult to fathom, and seems to suggest (she is not very explicit on the point) a downright circumvention of legality.[22] She sympathized with President Anzilotti's dissent, to the effect that the Court should have declined to give its opinion.

A decade later, in her Lauterpacht lectures (the lectures now being reissued under their original title *Legal Problems of International Organizations*), Morgenstern returned to the advisory opinion, and again invoked Anzilotti in support, but now on a different point. She now embraced Anzilotti's position that the Court had set the bar too high when deciding on Danzig. Anzilotti had pointed out, *ex abundante cautela*, that all that can be expected from a member state of the I.L.O. is that it complies with obligations of membership. Ratifying conventions may well be tempting, but is not an obligation; filing a complaint against another state may well be of interest, but is not an obligation. Hence, to insist on Poland's prior approval in such matters went too far, an opinion further supported, so Anzilotti pointed out, by the circumstance that several dominions and self-governing colonies had joined the I.L.O.[23]

In the mid-1970s, Morgenstern used the *Danzig/I.L.O.* opinion to illustrate the regrettable victory of politics over law. In the mid-1980s, she uses the same opinion (knowing full well it was hardly a classic — she mentions that it was "frequently forgotten") for a different purpose. To her 1980s mind, the *Danzig/I.L.O.* opinion seemed to entail two ramifications. First, there was a classic functionalist impulse: with most international organizations, there is merit in having as many members as possible, with all

[21] The idea of conceptual pluralism is borrowed from Hilary Putnam, *Ethics without Ontology* (Cambridge, MA: Harvard University Press, 2004).

[22] Felice Morgenstern, "Legality in International Organizations", 48 *B.Y.* 241-57 (1976–7), at 250-1.

[23] Felice Morgenstern, *Legal Problems of International Organizations* (Cambridge: Grotius, 1985), 47.

working to the same common goal. So why exclude anyone willing to join? This rested on a different interpretation of functionalism from the one entertained by the Court, with its seeming insistence that Danzig should only join if it could fully participate. Second, she was of course well aware that Danzig was not, in ordinary parlance and in strict legal terms, a state, but somehow did not care too much. What mattered was that it could conceivably assist the organization in the performance of some of its functions.

Thus put, Morgenstern clearly seems to stand in the functionalist tradition of legal scholarship as regards international organizations, but with a twist. Her work on international organizations law, strongly informed by her practical experiences as legal officer at the I.L.O., is difficult to capture in pre-existing theoretical terms: it carries traces of functionalism (it could hardly be otherwise, given functionalism's dominance), but also looks beyond functionalism, as her embrace of the Free City of Danzig suggests. It is no exaggeration perhaps to state that she developed her own way of thinking about international organizations, and, while she was difficult to pigeonhole, what is clear is that she was often ahead of her times.

E. On Legality

In the early 1950s, boasting glittering references from Sir Hersch Lauterpacht, a young Robbie Jennings and (then I.C.J. judge) Lord Arnold McNair, Morgenstern was appointed as legal officer at the I.L.O.[24] At the I.L.O., she did not write a great amount of academic work, but what she wrote was invariably worth reading, whether her writings on labour law, the substantive area of work of the I.L.O., or those concerning institutional law. She rose through the ranks and was in line to become the next legal adviser when she decided to seek early retirement. Upon her retirement, she continued to do some occasional work for the I.L.O., including representing the organization at the Vienna Conference on the Law of Treaties With or Between International Organizations. But mostly, it seems, she had chosen early retirement specifically with a view to preparing her Lauterpacht lectures, held in 1985 at Cambridge in honour of her mentor and teacher, Sir Hersch Lauterpacht, published a year later under the title *Legal Problems of International Organizations*.

While at the I.L.O., she wrote a few articles on aspects of international organizations law, the most important of which is most likely her contribution on legality. As with so much of her work, this was considerably ahead

[24] See, further, Klabbers, "The Timing".

of its time: writings on legality and related notions such as the rule of law in international organizations would only start to appear much later. The 'Legality' paper would pave the way for her later book, in that in it she tentatively started to explore an idea of international organizations as less than fully dependent on member states — less than fully functionalist. After all, a setting of legality differs, in principle, from one of member states instructing their organizations: legality presupposes something overarching.

Under 'legality', simply put, law reigns supreme, regardless of where it comes from. Under other approaches, the interests either of the member states or of the organization itself reign supreme; the law merely serves as an instrumental conduit for those interests. In speaking of legality, Morgenstern unleashed a unique and potentially very powerful mode of thinking about international organizations. Her tragedy (if that is the right word) was that her audiences were largely unable to see its potential. They could identify and respect her craftsmanship, her technical competence, but were not in a position properly to recognize the relevance of her work.

Still, it would be an exaggeration to suggest she had it all figured out and had developed a new theoretical framework for the law of international organizations. Like so many, she probably operated on the basis of intuition, gut feeling and socialization — and, throughout her work, the influence of Lauterpacht[25] and Jenks, her well-known I.L.O. colleague, can be seen.[26] Moreover, she was at times ambivalent, and understandably so. When suggesting that legality in international organizations derives from the organization's member states, she merely stated what seemed to be the obvious. After all, the law has to come from somewhere and, for a classically trained international lawyer (and given the absence of an omnipotent deity), that can only mean that the law needs to emanate from states. Still — and here she departed from more established ways of thinking about international organizations — once the law was in place and due respect was paid to considerations of discretion, it would lead a life of its own, guiding an increasingly autonomous organization.

Thus, she could suggest (without putting it in so many words) that there was something a little unseemly about using credentials procedures to channel the political behaviour of a member state, and she could more

[25] In *Legal Problems,* she recalled the "great impact" he had on her, "teaching me by example to question and seek constructive answers related to the evolution of the law", and sharing "his conviction that any approach to the future must be based on law and on the moral precepts underlying it": Morgenstern, *Legal Problems,* vii.

[26] Morgenstern and Jenks worked closely together, and she was the obvious person to write his obituary: Felice Morgenstern, "Wilfred Jenks in the I.L.O.", 46 *B.Y.* xv-xxx (1972-3).

generally insist on protecting the rights of a minority — this is entirely consonant with any 'legality' approach.[27] She recognized problems of legality long before others did, for instance when discussing collaboration between international organizations *inter se*. Ideally, so she suggested, this would require a proper legal basis, although she was savvy enough to realize that often such legal basis was lacking. Instead, collaboration would often "involve action by the organs of one organization admittedly going beyond the normal constitutional mandate of that organization".[28]

As a result, her legality concept, rudimentary as it was, is mostly important as a transitional concept. It allowed her to sidestep the traditional tug of war between the organization and its member states, in which functionalists typically take the organization's side while realists emphasize the member state side. And in doing so, it allowed her to posit organizations as actors in their own right, while acknowledging that international organizations operate in relative autonomy from their member states' desires, yet without, strange as this may sound, slavishly following the dictates of 'the international'.[29] She is, thus, best seen as a transitional theorist, paving the way for others thinking much, much later about the rule of law in international organizations,[30] and thinking much, much later, about organizations as autonomous actors.[31]

F. Legal Problems

Even if her essay on legality has been dubbed "one of the few real classics of the discipline",[32] her magnum opus is no doubt her Lauterpacht lectures, published under the innocuous and unpretentious title *Legal Problems of International Organizations*. The lectures covered three distinct topics: the legal environment of international organizations, issues of membership and participation, and standard-setting by international organizations. True to her vocation as a practitioner of international

[27] See, generally, Morgenstern, "Legality". [28] *Ibid.*, 251.

[29] This end of the spectrum is populated both by functionalists such as Schermers and by 'organicists' (for want of a better term) such as Seyersted. For discussions of their work in theoretical terms, see Jan Klabbers, "Schermers' Dilemma", 31 *European Journal of International Law* 565-82 (2020), and Jan Klabbers, "On Seyersted's *Common Law of International Organizations*", 5 *International Organizations Law Review* 381-90 (2008).

[30] Seminal is Jeremy Farrall, *United Nations Sanctions and the Rule of Law* (Cambridge University Press, 2007).

[31] See, e.g., Richard Collins and Nigel White (eds.), *International Organizations and the Idea of Autonomy* (Abingdon: Routledge, 2011).

[32] Jan Klabbers, "Introduction", in Jan Klabbers (ed.), *International Organizations* (Dartmouth: Ashgate, 2005), xi-xxv, xix.

organizations law, she predominantly treats a host of practical questions, without paying too much attention to theoretical questions, and without paying too much attention to significant contemporary events. Since the International Tin Council crisis started to unfold around the time of her original lectures, it makes sense that no reference to it was made just yet. Less understandable perhaps is the absence of other crucial events going to the heart of international organizations law, such as the 1980 *W.H.O./Egypt* advisory opinion of the I.C.J. revolving around the headquarters agreement between the W.H.O. and Egypt.[33] In this opinion, the I.C.J. realized that it could not make a choice between treating Egypt as an autonomous treaty partner of the W.H.O., protected by the *pacta sunt servanda* principle, and treating Egypt merely as the member state of the W.H.O. that it also is. This problem signified the bigger problem with the vacuum assumption: member states can simultaneously be third parties. It is, of course, possible that she decided that, since she was not going to discuss issues of headquarters agreements in any way, there was no need for her to address these developments at all — but somehow this seems too convenient, especially since she actually aims to discuss organizations in their legal environment.[34]

The book's title is innocuous — descriptively accurate (in that it addresses legal problems of international organizations), but not very catchy. Much the same applies to the table of contents, which makes clear that the book will discuss three issues, all of them often considered a little, well, boring perhaps. There are no references to sexy topics such as the accountability of international organizations for human rights violations; there is no particular attention to specific policies of international organizations and their effects, hotly debated as these were in other circles. Instead, Morgenstern offers a discussion of three seemingly dry topics — lawyer's law, if ever there was such a thing. Nor is the writing terribly catchy. Morgenstern is a business-like writer, getting to the point in a streamlined and organized manner, but there are few eye-catching phrases or *mots justes*. The writing is solid, precise and readable, but not particularly memorable.

What makes *Legal Problems* so fascinating then is the sense that it is out of step with much that was published at the time, and in some respects proved far ahead of Morgenstern's time. International organizations lawyers have traditionally conceptualized the international organization as something created by member states, and affecting only member

[33] *Interpretation of the Agreement of 25 March 1951 between the WHO and Egypt* (advisory opinion), [1980] ICJ Reports 73.

[34] Then again, contemporary commentators generally failed to recognize the principled significance of the *W.H.O./Egypt* opinion.

states — not even individuals or legal persons within those member states.[35] The mainstream approach assumes, as noted, a vacuum drawn around the organization and its member states — there simply is no world outside it.

Morgenstern broke through all this, and it is fair to say she provides an early push to the re-thinking of the discipline that slowly got under way during the 1990s.[36] *Legal Problems* is divided into three chapters, all somehow aiming to address the relations of international organizations to the outside world. The focus rests not so much on the member states (although these are not overlooked), but on the way international organizations stand in the world around them, and the sort of legal issues this generates. On specific topics, others had done some work. Studies had appeared on the legal personality of international organizations under international law, but international legal personality was usually considered to reflect the wishes of member states: it was up to the member states, so the discipline overwhelmingly held, to decide whether or not to endow their creation with personality under international law.[37] Likewise, there had been work on the treaty-making powers of international organizations since the mid- or late 1950s, but again the dominant idea was that this concerned powers that the member states had endowed their creation with.[38] After all, in this way it could be reconciled with the vacuum assumption: the external relations of international organizations, i.e. their connections to the world around them, could be reduced to an investigation of the competencies or characteristics the organizations had been given by their member states. And this, in turn, meant that the discipline could profess to afford not paying much attention to how those connections would work. Studies of treaty-making by international organizations to this day tend to focus on precisely those powers and their provenance, rather than on the

[35] The intellectual trajectory of international organizations law is traced in Klabbers, "The Transformation".

[36] During the 1990s, in the aftermath of the Tin Council crisis, negatively affecting third parties, the first studies appeared addressing the responsibility of international organizations as actors in their own right. One of the best is Moshe Hirsch, *The Responsibility of International Organizations toward Third Parties: Some Basic Principles* (Dordrecht: Martinus Nijhoff, 1995). The seminal discussion of the Tin Council crisis is Romana Sadurska and Christine Chinkin, "The Collapse of the International Tin Council: A Case of State Responsibility?", 30 *Virginia Journal of International Law* 845-90 (1990).

[37] For discussion, see Jan Klabbers, "Presumptive Personality: The European Union in International Law", in Martti Koskenniemi (ed.), *International Law Aspects of the European Union* (The Hague: Martinus Nijhoff, 1998), 231-53.

[38] See, e.g., J.W. Schneider, *Treaty-Making Power of International Organizations* (Geneva: Droz, 1959).

practice of treaty-making, the modalities of treaty-making, and other questions which involve the outside world.[39]

Morgenstern was, as far as can be ascertained, the first to go systematically beyond the 'vacuum view'. Whether she actively intended to do so remains unclear. She was not given to abstract theorizing, and made sure that her work would always be traceable to practical issues, to problems arising in practice. But if the *systematization* may have been unintentional, the move beyond the vacuum view was most assuredly intentional. The Introduction to *Legal Problems* highlights the role of international organizations in the conduct and management of international affairs, and the first chapter opens with the quip that "no organization is an island, entire of itself".[40] It cannot be emphasized enough that, while this appears a truism, it represents a fundamental change in register as far as international organizations law is concerned. In a discipline prone to viewing treaties (and therewith also international organizations) as "things between the parties" (*res inter alios acta*), to suggest that no organization is an island chips away at the very foundational assumptions of the discipline.

Legal Problems' three parts are roughly equal in size, with all three discussing aspects of international organizations law that are only conceivable on a view of international organizations that goes beyond the vacuum, beyond the relationship between the organization and its member states. Much of the academic study of international organizations was, and still is, overly state-centric, perhaps most obviously so amongst students of International Relations (for whom the work of international organizations is usually the simple result of member state preferences) but also among international lawyers. In the process, what is often ignored is that the organization operates with a degree of autonomy (however relative this autonomy may be) and within a particular force-field typically made up not only of member states, but also of civil society representatives, corporations, private persons and other international organizations. This realization now shines through in the three chapters of *Legal Problems.*

The first chapter is dedicated to a discussion of the legal environment in which international organizations operate. Morgenstern sketches whether the activities of international organizations are subject to international law, both public international law and private international law, and reaches the conclusion that on many points the law is uncertain. That was a valid conclusion when *Legal Problems* first came out, and is still a valid conclusion two decades into the twenty-first century, with discussions

[39] The leading study of the U.N.'s treaty practice dates back to the 1950s. See Shabtai Rosenne, "United Nations Treaty Practice", *R.C.A.D.I.* 1954-II, pp. 281-443.

[40] Morgenstern, *Legal Problems*, 3.

raging on such questions as whether international organizations are bound by customary international law,[41] or the question whether the internal rules of international organizations can themselves be considered part of international law.[42] Morgenstern, in this first chapter, also looks at how private international law may (or may not) apply, and, in her usual manner, here too the inspiration was practical, aiming to address and perhaps solve practical puzzles. One such puzzle pertains to the recognition of divorce of officials. In the absence (most likely) of internal rules of the organization, should this be guided by the law of the state of nationality of the official? Or the law of their state of residence? And what if these say different things: can guidance be derived from international treaties to which the organization itself is not a party, such as the 1970 Hague Convention on the Recognition of Divorce?

The point to note with respect to these questions is that they all presuppose that, indeed, no organization is an island — they presuppose that there are possible questions that cannot meaningfully be approached, much less answered, without accepting the proposition that there is a larger world in which the organization is embedded. Obvious though this may sound, it is a realization of the greatest relevance, for it marks a radical departure from the vacuum assumption mentioned above — the idea that the only legally relevant relationship is that between the organization and its member states. Morgenstern demonstrates compellingly that this assumption does not hold; she demonstrates convincingly that organizations operate in a world populated by non-member states, by other organizations, by staff members and by others, in such a way that those dealings cannot be reduced to the simple 'member state — international organization' dynamic.

The second chapter is devoted to the seemingly more sedate issue of participation in international organizations, and starts in classic fashion with a discussion of membership and how to acquire it. Here too, however, the vacuum assumption is eventually pierced: the chapter progressively includes discussions of the position of liberation movements, other international organizations, employers and employees (this could hardly be otherwise, in light of Morgenstern's lengthy involvement with the International Labour Organization), and non-governmental organizations.

[41] See, e.g., Jan Klabbers, "Sources of International Organizations' Law: Reflections on Accountability", in Samantha Besson and Jean d'Aspremont (eds.), *The Oxford Handbook of the Sources of International Law* (Oxford University Press, 2017), 987-1006; and Kristina Daugirdas, "How and Why International Law Binds International Organizations", 57 *Harvard Int'l L.J.* 325-81 (2016).

[42] Lorenzo Gasbarri, *The Concept of an International Organization in International Law* (Oxford University Press, 2021).

Curiously perhaps, there is an unresolved tension at the heart of the chapter. It is by some distance the most 'functionalist' in its tone: rules on participation, she writes, "should be designed to further the aims and purposes of the organization and the effectiveness of its work".[43] This is a typically functionalist point to make, the underlying idea being that the law should as far as possible facilitate the achievement of the organization's function. The curiosity then resides in the circumstance that, even assuming all member states have the same basic idea about the desirability and urgency of the organization's function, it is not always the case that this is shared by external actors. Put differently, an N.G.O. like Amnesty International may entertain different ideas about how the World Bank functions best than a fellow organization such as the International Monetary Fund. Employers and employees may have different ideas about how the I.L.O. can be successful, except perhaps on a high level of abstraction. In other words, the chapter still betrays a classic functionalist outlook, assuming that at the end of the day international organizations work for the common good, for the "salvation of mankind", and all reasonable people, whether employers or employees, N.G.O. activists or international officials, agree on what the common good consists of and how to get there.

Still, while such a conception is no longer tenable (despite its long pedigree), the remarkable thing about this second chapter is nonetheless that the functionalist perspective runs concurrent with the vacuum assumption being pierced. She does this when discussing the position of observers in international organizations, although to some extent this was a popular topic in the early 1980s, just before Morgenstern delivered her lectures.[44] But in discussing in more detail the various roles of observers and ensuing legal relations, she was little short of revolutionary, in particular perhaps when it comes to relations between international organizations *inter se.* The discipline as a whole only started to recognize this as a topic worth discussing during the 2010s, with useful studies being written by Boisson de Chazournes,[45] Lagrange,[46] Frid perhaps,[47] and

[43] Morgenstern, *Legal Problems,* 46.

[44] The leading studies are Eric Suy, "The Status of Observers in International Organizations", 160 *R.C.A.D.I.* 1978-II, pp. 75-179, and Sybesma-Knol, *The Status of Observers.*

[45] Laurence Boisson de Chazournes, *Interactions between Regional and Universal Organizations: A Legal Perspective* (Leiden: Martinus Nijhoff, 2017).

[46] Evelyne Lagrange "Les relations entre les organisations internationales", in Michele Vellano (ed.), *Il futuro delle organizzazioni internazionali: prospettive giuridiche* (Naples: Scientifica, 2015), 131-66.

[47] Frid's study dates from the mid-1990s and revolves around the E.U.'s position vis-à-vis other international organizations, a highly atypical setting. See Rachel

others.[48] Hence, in particular here, Morgenstern was far ahead of her time, a position facilitated no doubt by her practical experiences: she could observe first-hand what was going on between the I.L.O. and other international organizations. The questions may seem prosaic: how to accommodate organs of one organization in meetings of another? How to compose the sending organization's delegation? And below this lurk several other issues, none more so than how and by whom relationship agreements between organizations should be concluded, and whether there are general principles applicable to legal relations involving different international organizations. Some of those issues were only picked up later[49] or have yet to be picked up, but Morgenstern was the first to pay attention to them.

The third chapter seems, likewise, deceptively ordinary: an in-depth discussion of standard-setting by international organizations, divided into a section on law-making and one on non-binding standards. Again though, there is a novel element just below the surface: the realization that those standards aim to influence not so much the activities of member states, but rather those of actors within those member states. With respect to legally binding standards (few and far between, as few international organizations have proper law-making powers),[50] these may have to be set using the member states as conduits. These may be expected to transform the international standards into national legislation, for example. But Morgenstern also realizes that international organizations (above and beyond the E.U.) aim to directly influence the behaviour of individuals and companies. The chapter's title already provides a subtle hint in that direction: where the usual terminology speaks of 'law-making' or 'standard-setting' by international organizations, Morgenstern speaks of the "establishment of standards of conduct", and notes that many such standards are designed to "influence national law and practice".[51] More directly, she notes that recommendations "can be addressed to persons or

Frid, *The Relations between the EC and International Organizations: Legal Theory and Practice* (Dordrecht: Martinus Nijhoff, 1995).

48 René Uruena, "Interaction between International Organizations", in Jan Klabbers (ed.), *The Cambridge Companion to International Organizations Law* (Cambridge University Press, 2022), 222-43. The topic has also been discovered by International Relations scholars: see, e.g., Benjamin Faude, *Von Konkurrenz zu Arbeitsteilung: Komplexität und Dynamik im Zusammenspiel internationaler Institutionen* (Frankfurt: Campus, 2015); Jonas Tallberg et al. (eds.), *The Opening Up of International Organizations: Transnational Access in Global Governance* (Cambridge University Press, 2013).

49 By, in particular, Lagrange, "Les relations".

50 For a recent discussion, see José Alvarez, "Standard-setting in UN System Organizations", in Klabbers (ed.), *Cambridge Companion*, 120-46.

51 Morgenstern, *Legal Problems*, 92.

entities other than States",[52] thus making clear, once again, that she was well aware that there was more to the law of international organizations than merely the dynamic between the organization and its member states.[53]

In fact, with hindsight, there is even more to the law of international organizations than mere law, strictly speaking. While it remains an underdeveloped point in *Legal Problems* (and it is tempting to read too much into it), she draws attention to how international organizations promote compliance by providing assistance.[54] It is this assistance that has come to occupy a strong position in recent academic writings on governance by international organizations through experts and through epistemic means.[55]

G. To Conclude

It is not very plausible to suggest that Felice Morgenstern exercised a huge influence on the development of the law of international organizations. With her main work having been unavailable for quite some time, she is not cited all too often, and her h-index, a common (if flawed) measure of individual scholarly impact in the twenty-first century, would be on the low side. Her influence is bound to have been elsewhere, in particular perhaps as a mentor to younger colleagues within the legal department of the I.L.O.

And yet it is high time that *Legal Problems* is made available again. In part, this is because, first, it is, quite simply, a masterful work, providing subtle and sophisticated analyses of issues (legal problems, indeed) that have plagued international organizations law and continue to do so. Morgenstern rarely provides definitive answers, but her well-informed discussions are well worth reading and thinking about.

Second, there is the sheer joy of reading high-quality doctrinal scholarship, not driven by easy political opinion (although Morgenstern is neither politically innocent nor naïve) or by theory or method or other easy academic conceits, but driven by practical puzzles and concerns, approached by a strongly analytical mind sincerely searching for answers.

[52] *Ibid.*, 127.

[53] She had, in a similar vein, devoted an earlier article to international legislation, to a large extent covering the normative output of international organizations. See Felice Morgenstern, "International Legislation at the Crossroads", 49 *B.Y.* 101-17 (1978).

[54] *Ibid.*, 125.

[55] Guy Fiti Sinclair, *To Reform the World: International Organizations and the Making of Modern States* (Oxford University Press, 2017).

Legal Problems was not written to dazzle an audience and show how bright the author is; nor was it written to satisfy the demands of a funding agency, or in order to generate clicks and tweets. Therewith, Morgenstern's book — and Morgenstern herself — serve as a fine exemplar of what it means to engage in scholarly work.

But, most of all, *Legal Problems* should be available for wide reading because it was so far ahead of its time. As noted, while it is sometimes tempting to read too much into her work, she nonetheless repeatedly pierced the dominant vacuum assumption. Morgenstern drew attention to the provision of technical assistance as an important task of international organizations, and was the first to realize that the interaction between international organizations *inter se* would benefit from more professional attention by international organization lawyers.

International organizations are, by and large, the main institutions of global governance. International organizations regulate within their sphere of activity, they manage within their sphere of activity, and in the process distribute costs and benefits — on states, but also on actors within states. The role they play in everyday life, in global politics and in the global economy, should not be underestimated, and much of that role is itself embedded in a legal framework. Morgenstern was among the first to realize that the world of international organizations does not stop at the door of the member states, but that international organizations also penetrate inside those member states, affect all sorts of actors, and the law can only be understood on that basis. The future international organizations lawyer currently in law school or preparing for law school will have to come to terms with the broad reach of international organizations; having Felice Morgenstern's *Legal Problems of International Organizations* available should be of considerable help.

Preface

I was glad to have been invited to deliver the Hersch Lauterpacht lectures; very glad indeed for the opportunity it has given me to pay homage in a small way to someone whom I remember with respect, affection and gratitude. In preparing the lectures I was able to appreciate, once again, the great impact he had on my development and career, teaching me by example to question and to seek constructive answers related to the evolution of the law. And I say 'evolution' purposefully because in all his work he was aware that the world was changing too rapidly for any other approach to be valid. If I show less confidence in the future than he perhaps might have done, it may be because I do not have the same degree of courage as he did, or because the twenty-five years since his death have provided little ground for faith. I do share his conviction that any approach to the future must be based on law and on the moral precepts underlying it.

Two former colleagues who have remained friends, Mr Jacques Lemoine and Mr Nicolas Valticos, read large sections of the manuscript and gave me the benefit of their knowledge and reflection. I am grateful for the generosity with which they allowed me to benefit from their expertise and absolve them of responsibility both for my views and for any mistakes that may have escaped their vigilance.

My thanks also go to the Research Centre for International Law of the University of Cambridge and its Director, Mr Eli Lauterpacht, for the invitation to lecture, for all the preparation of the event and for making publication of the lectures possible; to Mr S.R. Pirrie, Mr H.E. Schade and Mrs M. DeVine for editorial assistance in connection with the publication; and to Mrs J. Kornhauser for preparing the index.

Last, but not least, I express my appreciation to the Library of the International Labour Office for access to the mass of paper in which the story of international organizations may be deciphered, and for the helpful patience of its staff.

Felice Morgenstern
August 1985

Abbreviations

A.J.I.L.	*American Journal of International Law*
Ann. Dig.	*Annual Digest and Reports of Public International Law Cases:* volumes 1–16 of the *International Law Reports*
Ann. Français	*Annuaire français de droit international*
Ann. Suisse	*Annuaire suisse de droit international*
B.Y.	*British Yearbook of International Law*
Canadian Yearbook	*Canadian Yearbook of International Law*
C.M.L.R.	*Common Market Law Review*
C.M.L. Reports	*Common Market Law Reports*
E.C.R.	*European Court Reports*
German Yearbook	*German Yearbook of International Law*
Harvard Int'l L.J	*Harvard International Law Journal*
I.C.J. Reports	*International Court of Justice Reports*
I.C.L.Q.	*The International and Comparative Law Quarterly*
I.L.O. Off. Bull.	*I.L.O. Official Bulletin*
I.L.R.	*International Law Reports* (earlier *Annual Digest and Reports of Public International Law Cases*)
Italian Yearbook	*Italian Yearbook of International Law*
J.I.L.E.	*Journal of International Law and Economics of George Washington University*
Journal officiel	*Journal officiel des Communautés Européenes*
Netherlands Int' Law Rev.	*Netherlands International Law Review*
Netherlands Yearbook	*Netherlands Yearbook of International Law*
P.C.I.J.	*Permanent Court of International Justice*
R.C.A.D.I.	*Recueil des Cours de l'Académie de droit international de la Haye*
Rev. crit.	*Revue critique de droit international privé*
Rev. esp.	*Revista espanola de derecho internacional*

R.G.D.I.P.	*Revue générale de droit international public*
Riv. dir. int.	*Rivista di diritto internationale*
U.N.J.Y.B.	*United Nations Juridical Yearbook*
Y.B.I.L.C.	*Yearbook of the International Law Commission*
Y.B.U.N.	*Yearbook of the United Nations*

Abbreviations of Organizations

A.C.C.	Administrative Committee on Co-ordination
E.C.	European Economic Community
E.C.O.S.O.C.	United Nations Economic and Social Council
E.C.S.C.	European Coal and Steel Community
Eurocontrol	European Organization for the Safety of Air Navigation
F.A.O.	Food and Agriculture Organization of the United Nations
G.A.	General Assembly of the United Nations
G.A.T.T.	General Agreement on Tariffs and Trade
I.A.E.A.	International Atomic Energy Agency
I.C.A.O.	International Civil Aviation Organization
I.C.E.M. (now I.C.M.)	Intergovernmental Committee for (European) Migration
I.C.J.	International Court of Justice
I.F.A.D.	International Fund for Agricultural Development
I.L.O.	International Labour Organization
I.M.F.	International Monetary Fund
I.M.O.	International Maritime Organization (formerly I.M.C.O., Intergovernmental Maritime Consultative Organization)
I.N.G.O.	International Non-Governmental Organization
INTERPOL	International Criminal Police Organization
I.T.U.	International Telecommunications Union
N.A.T.O.	North Atlantic Treaty Organization
O.A.U.	Organization of African Unity
O.E.C.D.	Organisation for Economic Co-operation and Development
P.A.H.O.	Pan American Health Organization

U.N.	United Nations
U.N.C.T.A.D.	United Nations Conference on Trade and Development
U.N.D.P.	United Nations Development Programme
U.N.E.P.	United Nations Environment Programme
U.N.E.S.C.O.	United Nations Educational, Scientific and Cultural Organization
U.N.I.T.A.R.	United Nations Institute for Training and Research
U.N.R.W.A.	United Nations Relief and Works Agency for Palestine Refugees
U.P.U.	Universal Postal Union
W.H.O.	World Health Organization
W.M.O.	World Meteorological Organization

Table of Cases

[References to pages in this volume are given in bold figures.]

Introduction

Nearly a quarter of a century has passed since the death of Sir Hersch Lauterpacht. At the time of his death, public international organizations were beginning to outnumber States, but no one foresaw the potential, both for growth and for variety, of that form of international activity; this may explain why he did not devote any major work to the place of international organizations in international law. At present, a considerably larger total of States is much more heavily outnumbered by the total of international organizations; a proportion of three to two is probably an unduly conservative estimate.

It is possible to take the view that there has been excessive proliferation of international bodies. The need for the continued existence of one or other such body may be open to question. What the numbers do suggest is that international relations can no longer function without the support of international organizations. Other *indicia* bear this out. For instance, referring to the return of the United States to the International Labour Organization less than three years after its withdrawal in 1977, a German author has commented that even a major power cannot now afford to turn its back on a body such as the I.L.O.[1] The fact that countries whose policies are regularly subjected to criticism in international organizations nevertheless seek to maintain their membership in them is also significant. Absence from international organizations is tantamount to isolation.

[1] H. Ballreich, "Die Interdependenz internationaler Organisationen", 19 *Archiv des Völkerrechts* 1980–1981, p. 121 at 122.

International organizations vary greatly. So, *pace* the principle of sovereign equality, do States. All States have certain features in common. The same cannot be categorically asserted of organizations, but at the very least they share certain categories of problems. To what extent does the law, and in particular international law, provide answers to these problems and, more generally, effectively regulate the functioning of bodies which have become indispensable participants in international life? Has international law kept abreast of the changing pattern of international activity?

It is proposed, in these lectures, to consider these questions in relation to three problem areas: the external relations of organizations; participation in their work; and their standard-setting activities. The issues to be examined within these areas will be limited to those of practical relevance to the operation of organizations; it should however be borne in mind that theoretical perceptions — of the nature of international organizations as subjects of international law and the character of their legal personality — influence responses to many of these issues. A further limitation concerns source material: it is difficult to be acquainted with the particular problems and rules of more than a small percentage of organizations; these tend to be the major universal and regional organizations.

1

The Legal Environment

During the formative period of international organizations, attention was largely[1] focused on their "internal" law, *i.e.* on their functions, powers and procedures under their constitutions and other rules. The assumption that international organizations do not have a common denominator encouraged such introspection. However — to misapply a famous quotation — no organization is an island, entire of itself. For their dealings with the outside world, whether in the sphere of public international law or in that of private law, the internal rules of organizations are relevant but not sufficient.[2]

General legal rules supplementing the internal law of organizations outside its proper sphere of application are little developed. This causes relatively few major problems, largely because practical arrangements circumventing open legal issues can usually be found. Nevertheless, the absence of accepted rules creates a climate of legal uncertainty. Recourse to arrangements evading the legal

[1] There have, of course, been major exceptions to this. For instance, in *The Proper Law of International Organizations* (1962), C.W. Jenks sought to elaborate the general principles applicable to various private law relations of international organizations. While, in a number of areas, it was (and remains) difficult to affirm what the law is, his statement of the issues which may arise is comprehensive. In recent literature, H.G. Schermers, *International Institutional Law* (2nd ed. 1980) deals extensively with the legal environment of international organizations.

[2] On the need for some general rules, applicable to all international organizations, concerning their external relations, see P. Reuter, "Sur quelques limites du droit des organisations internationales", *Festschrift für Rudolf Bindschedler* (1980), p. 491.

issues prevents the development of practice and hence of custom. If the legal environment in which organizations operate is not exactly hostile, it is certainly not well adapted to them.

A. Public International Law

Three major groups of questions regarding the place of international organizations in public international law require some consideration: to what extent are the rules of general international law suitable for application to international organizations; to what extent have rules of international law been evolved which are responsive to specific problems posed by international organizations; and in what manner can international law be made applicable to international organizations?

1. The Suitability of General International Law for International Organizations

"International law is essentially a law *between* States and this remains true in spite of the appearance of various international organizations . . ."[3] Large areas of international law are patently inapplicable to international organizations, which have no territory, confer no nationality and do not exercise jurisdiction in the same sense as States.[4] Other rules, while not as clearly inapplicable, either lack relevance to international organizations or meet practical difficulties of implementation. For instance, while questions regarding the succession of one international organization to another have arisen,[5] the law of State succession has not been noticeably pertinent. The United Nations has referred to such matters as absence of authority to exercise criminal jurisdiction over members of armed forces or of administrative competence relating to territorial sovereignty, to explain its inability as an organization — as opposed to the

[3] I. Brownlie, "The Reality and Efficacy of International Law", 52 *B.Y.* 1, 3 (1981).

[4] An international organization directly administering a territory may be regarded as exercising the functions of a government rather than performing the normal role of an organization.

[5] See, e.g., Cansacchi, "Identité et Continuité des sujets internationaux", 130 *R.C.A.D.I.* 1970-II, p. 1. The question of the possible succession of an international organization to the treaties of its member States is raised by the European Communities.

ability of national military contingents placed at its disposal — to apply detailed aspects of the law of war.[6] And, while it appears to be established that international organizations may not only bring international claims but that such claims may be brought against them, the absence of territorial jurisdiction and of institutional arrangements pertaining thereto make key concepts of State responsibility — such as the exhaustion of local remedies — inapplicable.[7]

Three main subjects are, *prima facie,* suitable for application to international organization: the law of State immunity; the law of diplomatic relations; and the law of treaties. It is no coincidence that the International Law Commission has been examining these subjects in that light. Yet the Commission has not found it easy to arrive at conclusions or to evolve agreed principles, whether paralleling or diverging from the law applicable to States. Answering, in 1970, the question why the Commission left open the application of many subjects to international organizations, one of its members at the time expressed the view that

> the more one looks at the Vienna Convention on the Law of Treaties, the more difficult it will be found to apply its provisions automatically to treaties of organizations. The same is true of other branches of the law. It was not an easy task to take the Vienna Convention of 1961 on Diplomatic Relations and adapt it to the peculiar requirements of ... Permanent Missions to international organizations ...[8]

Some of the specific difficulties will now be considered. In many cases, their potential solution is dependent not only on one or other concept of international organizations, but also on one or other explanation of the reasons for the rule binding on States.

(A) IMMUNITY

Overwhelmingly, the status of international organizations is regulated by treaties, whether they be constitutions, treaties between

[6] *U.N.J.Y.B.* 1972, p. 153. What was at issue was the possible acceptance by the United Nations of the Geneva Conventions; the arguments have, however, more general applicability.

[7] Some of the foregoing considerations must be qualified in relation to the European Communities.

[8] S. Rosenne, "The Role of the International Law Commission", *Proceedings of the American Society of International Law at its 64th Annual Meetings* 1970, p. 24 at 32.

States laying down general rules in the matter — such as the Conventions on the Privileges and Immunities of the United Nations and of the Specialized Agencies — or arrangements between particular organizations and countries in which their headquarters or other offices are established. Accordingly, the question whether international organizations enjoy immunity under customary international law has been marginal in the sense that it is liable to arise mainly where an organization is active in a non-Member State and no special arrangements have been concluded, or where treaty provisions are incomplete. There is some literature on the subject and there have been some court decisions favouring immunity in the absence of a treaty obligation;[9] such immunity has been variously justified on the ground of transfer of portions of State sovereignty or of State functions, or on the ground that an international body is by its nature, or the nature of its acts, not subject to national law.[10]

Since there is little reliance on the law of State immunity, there is uncertainty regarding the applicability and suitability of certain of its concepts. Thus, it has widely been assumed that the age-old problem of the delimitation of immunity from jurisdiction — of acts *iure imperii* and acts *iure gestionis* — has little application to international organizations (except where, as in the case of the World Bank, such immunity is expressly limited by reference to the nature of the activities of the organization). The assumption rests on two specific bases: first, many of the relevant treaties[11] provide for immunity from jurisdiction without any qualification; second, the fact that the capacity of international organizations is directly related to their public functions seems to imply that, as a matter of principle, the problem of acts *iure gestionis* should remain unimportant.[12] More generally, "absolute" immunity is justified by

[9] For a review of both, see F. Schröer, "De l'application de l'immunité jurisdictionnelle des Etats étrangers aux organisations internationales", 75 *R.G.D.I.P.* 712 (1971).

[10] See also *Y.B.I.L.C.* 1977-II, Part I, p. 152 for the views of the United Kingdom and Swiss Governments regarding general legal obligations in the matter.

[11] The Conventions on the Privileges and Immunities of the United Nations and the Specialized Agencies and the headquarters agreements of most major organizations. It should be added that there are headquarters agreements which give no immunity from jurisdiction to the organization as such.

[12] Would, for instance, the sweeping denial of immunity for contracts for the supply of goods under the United Kingdom State Immunity Act, 1978, be

the vulnerability of international organizations which have no territory of their own and thus necessarily operate within the jurisdiction of other legal systems, and the law of which is relatively little developed. When the Government of Italy in 1952 communicated to the Secretary-General of the United Nations a ratification of the Convention on the Privileges and Immunities of the Specialized Agencies accompanied by the statement that immunity from jurisdiction would be accorded to the agencies "insofar as said immunity is accorded to foreign States in accordance with international law", this was regarded by the agencies as a reservation and the instrument was, because of their objections, not accepted for deposit.

However, Italian Courts have always applied the distinction between acts *iure imperii* and acts *iure gestionis* to international organizations in the absence of treaty obligations relevant to the subject.[13] United States Courts have done so more recently[14] in a situation in which the only treaty providing for immunity from jurisdiction without qualification relates to the United Nations and national legislation (the International Organizations Immunities Act, 1945) specifically provides that international organizations enjoy the same immunity from suit and legal process as is enjoyed by foreign governments. In 1982, the Italian Court of Cassation went further: it applied the distinction to legal transactions by the F.A.O. in Italy, despite the fact that Section 16 of the headquarters agreement between that Organization and Italy provides for immunity from jurisdiction without qualification.[15] The

suitable for application to purchases by an organization of equipment for technical co-operation projects?

13 A key case was the decision of the Full Bench of the Court of Cassation in *Branno* v. *Ministry of War,* 22 *I.L.R.* 756. The case, which is also an example of the affirmation of immunity apart from treaty obligation, concerned N.A.T.O. The problem at issue was the provision of canteen facilities for staff.

14 See, e.g., *U.N.J.Y.B.* 1977, pp. 260-2. On the other hand, the effect on international organizations of the Foreign Sovereign Immunities Act 1976 has not yet been judicially determined. See R.P. Lewis, "Sovereign Immunity and International Organizations", *J.I.L.E.* 1979, p. 675, and the later decision of *Tuck* v. *P.A.H.O.*

15 The view that such treaty provisions did not affect a distinction considered by Italy to be a matter of customary international law had already been expressed by the Court in a 1976 case concerning I.C.E.M. (*U.N.J.Y.B.* 1973, pp. 197-8) and by a lower court in a 1969 decision concerning F.A.O. (*U.N.J.Y.B.* 1969, p. 238). However, in both cases the legal relationship in question (employer/employee) was held to be a matter of *iure imperii.*

Court eliminated the relevance of that provision to the case before it in part by holding that, in accordance with the rules usually applied to diplomatic immunity, it related only to the seat of the Organization. More generally, it affirmed that the extent of the immunity from legal process enjoyed by F.A.O. must be determined on the basis of the principles of international law developed in respect of the immunities enjoyed by foreign States.[16] It held a lease for offices to be a legal transaction *iure gestionis* on the ground that the "logistic" choice of accommodation is extraneous to the aims of the Organization and does not pertain to arrangements relating to the structure of the Organization. Both the F.A.O. Council[17] and the F.A.O. Conference have reacted by calling for the respect of the Organization's immunity "from all forms of legal process".[18] However, the representative of Italy to the 1983 Session of the Conference made it clear that the Court of Cassation would uphold its doctrine in any interpretation of internal law or treaty.[19] All parties seem resigned to concentrating on measures for immunity from execution. One may accordingly wonder whether other countries, including recent converts to limited immunity, will also move in that direction.

The question is all the more pertinent as the implementation of treaty obligations regarding the immunities of the staff of international organizations has tended to be influenced by the law applicable, between States, to diplomatic representatives. This is true, in particular as regards the grant of immunities to nationals. A number of countries have made express provision in or reservations to treaties on privileges and immunities of international organizations on this subject. In the case of the Convention on the Privileges and Immunities of the Specialized Agencies, ratifications subject to such reservations have not been registered and the countries concerned are not considered to be parties to the Convention. What is more significant, however, is that some countries treat their nationals differently from other staff members, in the absence of such provision or reservations, on the

[16] As seen by the court, the specific treaties would have had to make express exceptions to these principles if they were to be inapplicable.

[17] Resolutions 1/82 and 3/83. See also Doc. CL 82/5 (Report of the 42nd session of the Committee on Constitutional and Legal Matters) and Doc. CL 83/23.

[18] Report of the 22nd session of the conference, para. 345.

[19] *Ibid.*, para. 343.

apparent assumption that this is legally permissible.[20] For instance, Section 21 of the Convention on the Privileges and Immunities of the Specialized Agencies provides that, in addition to the functional immunities to be extended to all officials, "the executive head of each specialized agency, including any official acting on his behalf during his absence from duty, shall be accorded in respect of himself, his spouse and minor children, the privileges and immunities, exemptions and facilities accorded to diplomatic envoys, in accordance with international law". Section 15 of the United Kingdom Specialized Agencies of the United Nations (Immunities and Privileges) Order 1974, which gives effect to the Section in question, provides that it "shall not apply to any person who is a citizen of the United Kingdom and Colonies or a permanent resident of the United Kingdom".[21] The executive head would thus be limited to functional immunities, on the lines of the treatment of nationals under the Vienna Convention on Diplomatic Relations. It is permissible to wonder whether this was the intention of the phrase "in accordance with international law" in the Specialized Agencies Convention and, more fundamentally, whether it is appropriate that the status of the executive head of an organization, the exclusively international character of whose functions is recognized by Member States in pursuance of the constitution of the organization, and who frequently represents it in international relations, should be made dependent on his nationality. The statement accompanying the Italian ratification of the Convention, to the effect that Section 21 would be applied to officials of Italian nationality "with the same restrictions as are applicable, in accordance with international law, to diplomatic envoys of Italian nationality" was regarded by the organizations concerned as a reservation which, together with the one mentioned above,[22] has to date prevented registration of the ratification.

In 1980, the Administrative Committee on Co-ordination (consisting of the executive heads of all the organizations of the United Nations family) submitted a statement to the Economic and Social Council[23] in which it expressed its concern that certain States were

[20] Some developing countries do this as regards locally recruited, non-professional staff in offices on their territory, by reference to the wider question of categories of staff entitled to immunities.

[21] S.I. No. 1260, 1974. [22] See above p. 6. [23] U.N. Doc. E/1980/34, Add. 1.

denying the privileges of Section 21 of the Specialized Agencies Convention to their nationals by reference to Article 38 of the Vienna Convention:

> A.C.C. takes the view that the reference to international law in the relevant provisions of the Conventions on the Privileges and Immunities of the United Nations and the Specialized Agencies is meant to define the nature and extent of the additional privileges and immunities to be enjoyed, and not the persons to whom they apply. There is a fundamental difference between the status of diplomatic agents, as representatives of a State, ... and the status of international officials, as servants of the international community as a whole ... who must all be treated alike ... irrespective of their nationality. Indeed, when it framed Section 19 of the United Nations Convention (after which Section 21 of the Specialized Agencies Convention is patterned), the General Assembly rejected a proposal that States should have the right to limit the immunity of their nationals.
>
> While the number of cases involved is small, ... A.C.C. feels that it involves an issue of principle, inasmuch as this practice introduces an element of discrimination on grounds of nationality, which is contrary to ... the very concept of an independent international civil service ...

(B) DIPLOMATIC RELATIONS

International organizations frequently establish offices the purpose of which is to pursue relations with particular countries or other organizations. It has gradually become apparent that such offices have similarities with diplomatic missions in inter-State relations; for instance, the resident representatives of the United Nations Development Programme have been seen as an embryo of a diplomatic service of the United Nations family, while certain missions of the European Communities have been described as "Embassies".[24] The functions of such offices and representatives, while not identical to those of diplomatic missions, show analogies. There may have been some doubt as to whether the establishment of the office of an organization in a Member State requires the consent of that State,

[24] See, however, the second report of the Special Rapporteur on Relations between States and Inter-Governmental Organizations (*Y.B.I.L.C.*, 1967-II, p. 135) denying the "representative" character of persons connected with international organizations.

as the establishment of diplomatic relations would;[25] on the other hand, the assignment of particular officials to top relations posts is effectively subject to a form of "agrément", while any member of the "mission" of an international organization may be declared *persona non grata.*

Overwhelmingly, the States with which relations are established will be Members of the organization concerned (or, as in the case of U.N.D.P., of one or more of a group of organizations co-operating within a programme). Exceptionally, the issue may arise for a non-Member State. Thus, in 1982, the Direction du droit international public of the Swiss Federal Department of Foreign Affairs was called upon to give an opinion on the question whether a regional organization had a right of legation in relation to a non-Member State.[26] It took the view that this was dependent on the express or implied powers of the organization in question. It found that, while there was nothing express in the constitution of the organization concerned, its aims and purposes required some activity on the territory of non-Member States and from this concluded that the organization's active right of legation could not be denied. The establishment of relations with a particular country then required the latter's agreement. Given the exceptional nature of the issue, which meant that there could not be said to be customary international law on the subject, the opinion advised that a grant of rights in Switzerland called for parliamentary approval because they represented "new obligations".[27]

More attention has been paid to the accreditation of missions by States to international organizations. Again — as is expressly stated in Article 5 of the Vienna Convention on the Representation of States in their Relations with International Organizations of a Universal Character — the possibility of establishing such missions is in theory made dependent on the rules of the organization concerned. Since this is a matter generally not dealt with in express rules, the law has in fact developed as a result of practice. It was

[25] The doubt derives in part from the fact that the functions of such an office are not necessarily directed towards relations with that State.

[26] L. Caflisch, "La Pratique Suisse en matière de droit international public", 38 *Ann. Suisse* 1982, p. 69 at 110-15.

[27] In 1955 the United Kingdom adopted special legislation, the European Coal and Steel Community Act (4 Eliz. 2, ch. 4), to give status to a mission of the E.C.S.C.

perhaps to be expected that the establishment of a permanent mission by a Member State would not be subject to the consent of the organization; as indicated in the preamble to General Assembly Resolution 257(III)A, "the presence of ... permanent missions serves ... to keep the necessary liaison between the Member States and the Secretariat in periods between sessions of the different organs of the United Nations".[28] The same was not necessarily true in relation to non-Member States. In connection with the preparation of the Vienna Convention, a number of countries, including the United Kingdom, expressed the view that the establishment of permanent observer missions by non-Member States should be subject to the consent of the organization.[29] However, practice has been more lax and notifications of the establishment of such missions have frequently been simply accepted.[30] This is reflected in the final text of Article 5 of the Vienna Convention which permits the establishment of permanent missions by Members and of permanent observer missions by non-Members on the same legal footing, without any apparent need for consent.

The question then arises whether the appointment of a particular person as permanent representative or observer is subject to the *agrément* of the organization and whether, conversely, the organization is in a position to declare a representative or observer *persona non grata*. When the matter of permanent missions was considered at the third session of the General Assembly there was a controversial suggestion that their "credentials" be considered by the Credentials Committee of the Assembly; however, the resolution finally adopted provides only for an annual report of the Secretary-General on the credentials of permanent representatives. Practice does not suggest that this is used to give formal approval to appointments and no such approval is envisaged by the Vienna Convention, which provides that the credentials of the head of mission "shall be transmitted to the organization". As regards the converse problem, a legal opinion given to the Secretary-General of the United

[28] For the text see, *Y.B.U.N.* 1948-49, p. 973. For a view that liaison with a technical organization may be better achieved by the competent service in the sending State see *Y.B.I.L.C.* 1971-II, Part I, p. 427.

[29] The United Kingdom would also have required the consent of the host State.

[30] As regards the Holy See in the I.L.O., see Minutes of the 170th Session of the Governing Body (November 1967), p. 142; as regards W.H.O., see *Y.B.I.L.C.* 1971-II, Part I, p. 420.

Nations[31] took the view that there would be warrant for intervention by the United Nations in case of activities by members of a mission which did not pertain to the proper functions of the mission. In such a case, it would be for the Secretary-General to make representations to the State concerned; if these did not achieve satisfactory results, the matter might be brought before the General Assembly. There is nothing on the subject in the Vienna Convention. While there have been some cases of involuntary departure of members of permanent missions, this has usually occurred at the initiative of and for reasons primarily of concern to the host State. It is accordingly difficult to affirm that organizations may, for reasons of their own, declare a member of a permanent mission *persona non grata*.

What, of course, most differentiates relations between States and organizations from inter-State relations is the necessary involvement of a third party, the State in which the organization has its headquarters. This involvement raises two questions, that of the extent of the privileges and immunities which the host State is bound to grant, and that of the manner of protecting the legitimate interests of the host State. It may well be that under general international law regarding State immunity a certain status for representatives of a State is assured even in the absence of a treaty. Similarly, it may be that general rules derived from the independence and sovereignty of States require respect for the interests of the host State. However, the application of general principles to new phenomena requires some definition. Many of the instruments concerning the privileges and immunities of organizations contain provisions on State representatives which were drafted mainly with temporary presence in the host State in mind. As regards universal organizations, the Vienna Convention on the Representation of States has sought to cover the ground comprehensively. It would appear, however, that the major host States consider privileges and immunities granted under the Convention to be defined too extensively,[32] and their powers to react to non-compliance with the

[31] See *Y.B.I.L.C.* 1967-II, p. 165.

[32] J.P. Ritter, "La Conférence et la Convention sur la Représentation des États dans leurs Relations avec les organisations internationales", 21 *Ann. Français* 1975, p. 471, refers in particular to the provisions on accommodation for members of missions, on the status of members, and on the possible start of privileges prior to notification to the host State, as points considered objectionable. Of these, the

obligations of missions to be circumscribed too severely;[33] not one of them has to date ratified the Convention. This suggests that there is as yet no international consensus on the details of the law governing the status of the representation of States in relation to international organizations.

(C) TREATIES[34]

There are a number of theories regarding the basis of a treaty-making capacity of international organizations. The draft provision on the subject elaborated by the International Law Commission — "The capacity of an international organization to conclude treaties is governed by the relevant rules of that organization" — is stated in the Commentary to be a compromise, compatible both with the view that capacity derives from a principle of international law which can be modified only by express restrictive provisions of constituent instruments, and with the view that capacity is exclusively dependent on the rules of the organization concerned.[35] As has been pointed out[36] the main practical difference between these two approaches may be that, in the latter case and particularly

one on accommodation goes beyond the requirements — on a reciprocal basis — of the 1961 Convention on Diplomatic Relations. See also the expression of similar views by J.G. Fennessy, "The 1975 Vienna Convention on the Representation of States in their Relations with International Organizations of a Universal Character", 70 *A.J.I.L.* 62 (1976).

33 The text eschews the notion of "*persona non grata*". It permits the host State to take "such measures as are necessary for its own protection," in consultation with the sending State, "in order to ensure that such measures do not interfere with the normal functioning of the mission", and with the approval of the Foreign Minister of the host State.

34 All references in this Section to provisions elaborated by the International Law Commission refer to the draft articles on the law of treaties between States and international organizations or between international organizations, submitted to the General Assembly in 1982.

35 Report of the International Law Commission on the work of its 34th Session, Official Records of the General Assembly, 37th Session, Supplement no. 10 (hereinafter referred to as A/37/10), p. 41. A similar compromise was reached by the Institute of International Law in 1973; however, the resolution then adopted refers both to the rules of the organization and to "general practice in this field" and it was made clear that the practice in question might be that of other organizations.

36 M. Rama-Montaldo, "International Legal Personality and Implied Powers of International Organizations", 44 *B.Y.* 111, 1970.

where there are no express provisions,[37] there always remains room for argument whether the power exists. It would not seem that this is a major problem in relation to the other party with which a treaty may be concluded. Except for some discussion regarding the participation of the European Communities in certain multilateral Conventions,[38] challenge to the capacity of an international organization to enter into treaty relations with a State or another organization is a rarity.[39] At the same time a commitment of the organization is a constraint on the decision-making power of its organs and hence, indirectly, of its Members; there may also be liability for breach of the commitment. While, again, this has not so far given rise to particular difficulty, the fact that there are rarely express rules either on treaty-making capacity or on the organ exercising treaty-making powers leaves considerable room for internal controversy on the constitutionality of particular treaties.

Of perhaps more immediate practical relevance is the question which agreements concluded by international organizations with States or other organizations are in fact governed by international law. The problem is known also in inter-State relations: for instance, a number of States consider that so-called interdepartmental agreements are matters of private law. However, as regards international organizations there are at present no criteria for classifying agreements and there is apparently little practice of including express provisions clarifying the issue. In its comments on the definition of a treaty as "an international agreement governed by international law", the International Law Commission recognizes the existence of the problem: while stating that the draft articles do not purport to

[37] Reliance on the practice of organizations, in general or as part of the "rules" of the organization concerned, is liable to pose the question whether it remains eternally possible to contest the constitutionality of a settled practice or, conversely, whether practice can serve, by a process of interpretation, to develop and hence to some degree modify a constitution. For an examination of the views of the International Court on this issue, see E. Lauterpacht, "The Development of the Law of International Organization by the Decisions of International Tribunals", 153 *R.C.A.D.I.* 1976-IV, p. 380.

[38] See R. Kovar, "La participation de la C.E.E. aux conventions multilaterales", 21 *Ann. Français* 1975, p. 903. Reservations of the U.S.S.R. regarding commodity agreements, for instance, suggest that recognition of the E.E.C. rather than its treaty-making power, has been at issue.

[39] See below, p. 22 for a reference to G.A.T.T.'s capacity to conclude a headquarters agreement; the issue, in fact, was its personality.

provide criteria for determining whether an agreement between international organizations or between a State and an international organization is or is not governed by international law, since this depends essentially on the will of the parties, it does suggest that, where an agreement is concluded by an organization with recognized capacity to enter into agreements under international law and where that agreement is not by virtue of its purpose and terms of implementation made subject either to the national law of any State or to the rules of an organization, it may be assumed that the parties to the agreement intended it to be governed by general international law.[40]

Once we are dealing with "treaties", to what extent do the general rules of the law of treaties, as codified in the Vienna Convention of 1969 on the subject, apply? Again, there are two main approaches. One, which stresses the difference between States as primary and organizations as derivative subjects of international law, would wish the applicability of each rule to international organizations to be demonstrated. The other, exemplified by the United Kingdom,[41] establishes a presumption that once two entities having international capacity are validly in treaty relations with one another their rights as contracting partners are equal "and this presumption must stand unless there are clear reasons, in a particular set of circumstances, for drawing distinctions based upon the character and status of the parties".

Four main issues remain highly controversial.[42] One is the question whether the internal law of organizations, and particularly

[40] Report of the International Law Commission 1982 in U.N. Doc. A/37/10, pp. 28-9. A related question is whether the agreement has in fact been concluded by the organization as such. This issue arose, for instance, in respect of the relationship agreement between the E.E.C. and the I.L.O., entered into by the E.E.C. Commission; it was suggested by some that the agreement related only to the activities of the Commission and not to those of other E.E.C. organs. The question is, in turn, related to but distinct from that of the organs of an organization having treaty-making powers.

[41] See the United Kingdom comments on the first draft of the International Law Commission articles, *Y.B.I.L.C.* 1981-II, Part II, p. 191.

[42] There are other, more secondary, questions. One is the distinction drawn by the International Law Commission between "full powers" for representatives of States and "powers" for representatives of organizations, on the ground that organizations have circumscribed powers. The United Nations has suggested, in its comments (U.N. Doc. A/38/145, Add. 1, p. 20), that "full" powers refer not to the extent of the powers of the principal, but to the extent to which whatever

their constitutional law, can be equated with the internal law of States. A State may invoke the fact that its consent to be bound by a treaty has been expressed in violation of a provision of its internal law regarding competence to conclude treaties to invalidate its consent only if the violation was manifest and concerned a rule of internal law of fundamental importance. It may not invoke the provisions of its internal law as justification for its failure to perform a treaty at all. The International Law Commission finally opted for the application of parallel rules to organizations. However, a number of States and organizations continue to argue that, insofar as the internal law of an organization is itself a treaty, the position of an organization is entirely different. As regards the United Nations the issue is sharpened by Article 103 of the Charter which makes obligations thereunder prevail over other treaties.[43] It has also been suggested that there may be differences according to whether agreements are with Members or with non-Member States. An ancillary question to which the problem is of relevance is whether an organization may be considered, by reason of its conduct, to have acquiesced in the validity of a treaty, when the conduct was itself unconstitutional. Experience, as yet, provides no guidance.[44]

A second issue concerns the power of organizations to make reservations to treaties and to object to or accept reservations made by others. One suspects that an inclination to treat organizations differently from States in this respect derives from the view that reservations have their basis in the sovereignty of States, although early proposals of the International Law Commission, which provided for different treatment, were more subtly justified. However

powers the principal has are given to the agent. But it has taken the Holy See, with centuries of experience in putting princes in their place, to comment that even States do not enjoy "full" powers. (*Ibid.*, p. 8.)

[43] By its terms Article 103 deals with the obligations of Member States under the Charter and under other treaties. In its comments on Article 30 of the draft articles (successive treaties relating to the same subject-matter) the International Law Commission indicates that it did not arrive at a firm conclusion as to whether Article 103 applies also to treaties of organizations.

[44] See, however, Article 4(6) of Annex IX of the U.N. Convention on the Law of the Sea, which provides that "in the event of a conflict between the obligations of an international organization under this Convention and its obligations under the agreement establishing the organization or any acts relating to it, the obligations under this Convention shall prevail".

that may be, the final draft articles would treat organizations differently only in respect of the tacit acceptance of reservations. A number of comments made on the final draft suggest that even this distinction is not necessary. Such little practice as there has been — relating mainly to the treatment by the specialized agencies, as rather particular parties[45] to the Convention on the Privileges and Immunities of the Specialized Agencies, of reservations to that Convention — has involved both objections to substantive reservations and acceptance of procedural ones, without major challenge.

A third problem is that of the manner of creating rights and obligations for Member States through the conclusion of treaties by the organization. Draft article 36 *bis*, requiring the individual consent of Member States, appears to have been drafted primarily with the European Communities in mind. Its unsuitability in relation to universal organizations is suggested in a paper presented to the Sixth Committee of the General Assembly by the Administrative Committee on Co-ordination:

> Thus, [the] draft article cannot be applied, *inter alia*, to headquarters and conference agreements that create both rights and obligations for States which are not parties to them and whose individual consent is neither sought nor given. Moreover, were it to be provided that, in the absence of constitutional provisions to that effect, States members of an international organization can be bound by a treaty concluded by that organization only by their unanimous consent, it should be borne in mind that neither the United Nations Charter nor the constitutions of the specialized and related agencies provide for a unanimity rule.[46]

Some other, perhaps more fundamental, issues are involved in the controversy: for instance, to what extent do treaties of an organization create international rights and obligations directly between the other contracting parties and the Member States of the organization; and what relevance attaches to the manner in which and extent to which the Member States of an organization are liable for its obligations?[47]

[45] See below, p. 35f. [46] Doc. A/C.6/38/4 of 27 October 1983, para. 18.

[47] The Institute of International Law, in a resolution adopted in 1973 (*Annuaire de l'Institut de droit international*, 1973, pp. 797-8), left open the question of the obligations that might arise for Member States from treaties of the organization either under the rules of the organization or under a general rule of international law. One of the proposals submitted to it by its Rapporteur (R.J.

A final question is that of the scope of the commitment of international organizations. States bind themselves in respect of their entire territory unless a different intention appears from the treaty or is otherwise established. As regards organizations, the coverage of subsidiary and related bodies is at issue. It will be discussed in the next section.

By reference to the diversity of the present treaty practice of organizations and to the fact that law in the matter is comparatively recent and fragmentary and continues to evolve, as well as to the procedural difficulties (to be considered below) of making new rules applicable, the Administrative Committee on Co-ordination in the above-mentioned paper took the highly unusual step of suggesting to the General Assembly of the United Nations that it should not proceed in the immediate with the adoption of a formal convention on the subject; this would allow "the acquisition of relevant experience as well as the further development and gradual crystallization of this area of the law, which as yet does not appear ready for codification".[48] The General Assembly, while deciding in principle on a plenipotentiary conference "to be convened not earlier than 1985", continues to have the matter under advisement.*

2. *Specific Problems posed by International Organizations*

As indicated at the outset of this Chapter, rules of general international law are needed for specific problems of international organizations which cannot be answered by the internal law of

Dupuy) would have established a parallel between the power of an organization to create obligations for its Members by external and by internal action. Another would have required Members not to interfere with the implementation of a properly concluded treaty. An interesting example of the latter issue is discussed in H.J. Geiser, *Les effets des accords conclus par les organisations internationales* (1977), pp. 76-90: following a problem which arose in 1963 (*U.N.J.Y.B.* 1963, pp. 164-6) the question was put to Member States of the United Nations whether they would be prepared not to request the extradition from a host State of the organization of persons in that State in response to a U.N. invitation, seeing that the host State was required, under an agreement with the organization, to facilitate their attendance; a substantial number of States replied affirmatively.

48 Doc. A/C.6/38/4, para. 19.

* [Author's note: After these lectures were delivered, the General Assembly decided, by Res. 39/86, to hold a codification conference in February-March 1986.]

organization alone. One of these is basic: what is an international organization? Another relates to the legal aspects of relations between organizations.

(A) THE DEFINITION OF PUBLIC INTERNATIONAL ORGANIZATIONS

Two inter-related issues arise in international law: which corporate bodies operating in the international sphere may be regarded as public international organizations; and which such bodies have international legal personality, *i.e.* the capacity to exercise rights and assume obligations under international law. Internal law is unhelpful in the sense that, while many constitutions of such bodies provide for their legal personality, those that make it clear that international personality is intended can be counted on the fingers of one hand. Practice is confused and the fact that the matter is examined and conclusions are arrived at for widely different purposes makes generalizations difficult.

It is generally considered that in order to be regarded as an international organization and to have some personality in international law a body must be established by a treaty between States and States must be Members.[49] Practice may be making a number of inroads into that position.

Thus, the participation of existing international organizations in agreements establishing new international bodies is beginning to be accepted. In its Opinion 1/76 concerning the *Draft Agreement Establishing a European Fund for the Laying-up of Inland Waterway Vessels*[50] the Court of Justice of the European Communities *affirmed* that the European Economic Community had the capacity, in an area in which it assumed authority over external relations for the realization of one of the objectives of the Community, to co-operate with a third State in setting up a public international body and to give such body appropriate decision-making powers.[51] Another example, of interest because of the affirmation that the body

[49] The Vienna Codification Conventions define "international organizations" as "intergovernmental".

[50] (Case 1/76) [1977] E.C.R. 741.

[51] Furthermore, the Court considered it to be a necessary corollary of the internal distribution of powers in the Community that the Community and its institutions would, as such, participate with full membership rights in a body so created.

created does indeed have capacity in the sphere of international law, is that of the establishment of the U.N. Demographic Centre in Bucharest. The 1974 Agreement between the United Nations and Romania establishing the Centre specifies in Article I, Section 5, that the Centre has "legal personality distinct from that of the parties and shall not be considered as a body of the United Nations or of the Government".[52] The legal personality referred to could have been intended to be limited to the sphere of private law, particularly as a final sentence of the section provides that the Government shall publish statutory orders concerning the legal status of the Centre. The Director of the Centre accordingly sought guidance. In an opinion of March 1975 the United Nations Office of Legal Affairs took the view that

> considering that both Parties to the Agreement are themselves international entities, and since there is no indication to the contrary, the normal interpretation of Section 5 is that the Parties intended to confer international legal personality on the Centre . . . the exact attributes of the Centre's international legal personality would be defined by, or derive from, the terms and purposes of the Agreement, and it is this personality which, in turn, the Romanian Government would recognize and the acts of which it would regulate for the purposes of Romanian internal law in the regulations referred to in the last sentence of Section 5.[53]

Also, there are suggestions that international agreement to establish international persons need not take the form of a treaty, or indeed be concluded at the governmental level. There are examples of international organizations being established by conferences, without formal treaty.[54] The World Tourism Organization came into being as a result of government acceptances of a statute elaborated in 1970 by its non-governmental predecessor, the International

[52] *U.N.J.Y.B.* 1974, p. 25.

[53] *U.N.J.Y.B.* 1975, pp. 159-60. See also the 1974 Agreement between France and U.N.E.S.C.O. concerning the establishment and operation of an international Centre for registering serial publications (*Journal officiel*, March 1976, p. 1398), Article 4 of which provides for the "legal personality" of the Centre.

[54] The examples commonly given are those of the Colombo Plan Council and the Asian-African Legal Consultative Committee. Where a Conference resolution calls for ratification of a constitution (e.g. in the case of the Arab Labour Organization) the procedure is close to that of the negotiation of a treaty. See also W. Dale. "Is the Commonwealth an International Organization?", 31 *I.C.L.Q.* 451 (1982).

Union of Official Travel Organizations.[55] The Nordic Council, established by parallel parliamentary decisions and composed of parliamentarians, is regarded by many — though not by all — as an international organization.[56] Most provocative is a 1971 United Nations legal opinion on the establishment of a clearing union by the central banks of a number of Asian countries: after referring to Latin American and African precedents and remarking on the inappropriateness of making an agreement regarding such a union subject to the law of a particular country, the opinion suggests that

> [t]he principle that an international legal person can be created by virtue of a treaty is, after all, nothing more than a rule of customary international law, and it may well be that a new customary rule of international law is emerging under which such a legal person could also be created by an agreement concluded solely by autonomous public entities, such an agreement being governed by international law pursuant to another new customary rule . . .[57]

Whatever may be the merits of that suggestion the question of the status of bodies set up by and composed of public entities is posed in other contexts as well; it has arisen, for instance, as regards INTERPOL and as regards certain organizations composed in whole or in part of social security institutions.[58] The question is related to the effect, in international law, of so-called inter-departmental agreements. There is now perhaps a certain flexibility of approach to such forms of public international co-operation.[59]

[55] For a detailed description of the procedure followed see J. Castañeda, "Une nouvelle méthode pour la création d'organismes internationaux. Le cas récent de L'U.I.O.O.T.", 16 *Ann. Français* 1970, p. 625. See also R. Gilmour, "The World Tourism Organization: International Constitutional Law with a Difference", 18 *Netherlands Int' Law Rev.* 275 (1971).

[56] But the Inter-Parliamentary Union is not so regarded. H.G. Schermers (see p. 3, note 1 above) considers that the difference lies in the fact that governments participate in the work of the Nordic Council. Also, it now operates in the framework of the Treaty of Co-operation between Scandinavian Governments concluded in 1962 and amended in 1971, and is paralleled, in that framework, by the Nordic Council of Ministers.

[57] *U.N.J.Y.B.* 1971, 215 at 218. The conclusion may be denied by those who believe that only States can create international custom.

[58] For an examination of some borderline cases see M. Pérez González, "Las organizaciones no gubernamentales en el ambito de la organizacion internacional", 29 *Rev. esp.* 229 (1976). INTERPOL has, after lengthy consideration, been classified by the United Nations as an intergovernmental organization.

[59] See, for instance, "Netherlands State Practice for the Parliamentary Year 1979-80", 12 *Netherlands Yearbook* 165, 178 (1981), for a government explanation of

A second element generally referred to in order to determine whether a body is an international organization and has international personality is that of possessing organs and powers which are its own, as distinct from those of Member States. The problem here, in practice, is to decide where the border between legal dependence and independence lies.

The matter has been of particular importance in recent years in Switzerland because of the adoption of constitutional provisions making accession to or participation in the work of an international organization subject to referendum. Thus it was concluded in 1979 that accession to the International Whaling Convention of 1946 was not subject to referendum because the International Whaling Commission was a body common to the States Parties to the Convention, which expressed their collective will, and not a separate legal entity.[60] The fineness of the distinctions involved and the circular nature of relevant arguments are, however, best illustrated by an opinion on the legal personality of G.A.T.T.[61] It notes the institutional development of G.A.T.T. which, at the outset no more than a treaty, acquired organs after the projected International Trade Organization failed to come into being. It notes further that some authors consider that, by virtue of this development, G.A.T.T. has become a true international organization. Nevertheless, it concludes that G.A.T.T., although *in fact* an international organization because it has organs and a Secretariat, is not an organization *in law* because it has no personality distinct from the Member States and no independent legal will.

the need so to define international organizations in national constitutional documents that account can be taken of developments in the law. "Generally speaking, international public law organizations are taken to be organizations whose membership consists of States and which are brought into being by, or by virtue of, agreements; in addition to these, international law may also recognise other bodies as 'organizations based on international law'." (*Ibid.*)

60 L. Caflisch, "La pratique Suisse en matière de droit international public 1979", 36 *Ann. Suisse* 1980, p. 139 at 145-50; see also 34 *Ann. Suisse* 1978, p. 49 at 89-94, and 35 *Ann. Suisse* 1979, p. 117 at 132-3.

61 L. Caflisch, "La pratique Suisse en matière de droit international public 1978", 34 *Ann. Suisse* 1978, p. 49 at 83-7. The practical issue here was the conclusion of a headquarters agreement. The practical suggestion was that the Director-General of G.A.T.T. might conclude the agreement in the name and on behalf of the Contracting Parties. Consideration of the international personality of G.A.T.T. has been complicated by the fact that it has also acted as the Interim Committee of the still-born International Trade Organization.

If a "primary" international organization is not necessarily recognizable at sight, more difficult questions are raised by the status of certain "subsidiary" bodies established by majority decision of the organs of existing international organizations. A very substantial number of subsidiary organs has been created by various international organizations and indeed by existing subsidiary bodies.[62] Their nature, size and permanence varies greatly. The ones of more direct interest in the present context are those given "autonomy" or certain forms of legal capacity which leave ambiguous the legal sphere in which the capacity is to be exercised.

Some subsidiary bodies, for instance of the United Nations,[63] conclude agreements with governments and with other international organizations. This poses the question of the parties to the agreement, in other words, whether the subsidiary alone or the parent organization is bound by and responsible for the due performance of the agreement. The question has theoretical significance because of the light a treaty-making power may shed on the international personality of the body concerned.[64] It has practical implications, particularly when it is recalled that a frequent purpose of the establishment of subsidiary bodies is to separate their finances, largely based on voluntary contributions, from those of the parent organization. The Special Rapporteur of the International Law Commission, on the subject of treaties between States and International Organizations, P. Reuter, found ten years ago[65] that there was uncertainty both as to the legal status of subsidiary bodies and regarding the identification of the party to an agreement concluded by a subsidiary body; he was not certain

[62] Some bodies regarded as "subsidiary" have been established by independent bodies.

[63] They appear to be taken to exercise the treaty-making power of the United Nations: their agreements are registered, apparently under the provision of the relevant regulations which permit registration of treaties to which the United Nations is a party, and, insofar as they relate to privileges and immunities, published in the *United Nations Juridical Yearbook* under the heading of agreements relating to the status of the United Nations (with the curious exception of the agreement signed in 1975 between U.N.E.P. and Kenya).

[64] For an example of a subsidiary body being treated as a "third party" see the headquarters agreement of the International Agency for Research on Cancer. The Agreement is concluded by France and W.H.O., but Article XXII requires the approval of the Agency. (*U.N.J.Y.B.* 1970, pp. 41-5.)

[65] Second Report, *Y.B.I.L.C.* 1973-II, pp. 85-6.

whether it was useful or expedient to seek definition with a view to the greater security for other parties. In 1982, when finalizing articles on that subject, the Commission found itself in the same dilemma:

It would be useful to make it clear that, unless there is a properly established indication to the contrary, when an international organization binds itself by treaty, it also binds [all the entities, subsidiary organs, connected organs and related bodies which come within the orbit of that international organization and are incorporated in it to a greater or lesser extent]. Conversely, a treaty concluded on behalf of a subsidiary organ should bind the entire organization as well. However ... [t]his is an area in which notions, vocabulary and the practice of international organizations are not settled, and it seemed wisest to leave aside a subject which [it] is too early to codify.[66]

The question of the legal nature of subsidiary bodies also arises in connection with their ability to rely on arrangements for the privileges and immunities of the parent organization. There have been instances of the affirmation, in this connection, of the legal independence of certain bodies. For instance, in a legal analysis of U.N.R.W.A. a former legal adviser of that body cites two decisions of Egyptian courts affirming that it had juridical personality. In the first (*Husseini* v. *U.N.R.W.A. Representative*, 1957) a Court in Gaza reasoned that, as the Agency and not the United Nations had entered into international agreements with the Egyptian Government relating to the Gaza strip, U.N.R.W.A. "had a juridical personality independent from that of the United Nations" and held that the Convention on the Privileges and Immunities of the United

[66] Report of the International Law Commission on the work of its 34th Session, General Assembly, Official Records, 37th Session Supplement No. 10, p. 80. An example of the ambiguous nature of the treaty-making power of certain subsidiary bodies is provided by the Charter of the United Nations University, adopted by General Assembly Res. 3081 (XXVII) on 6 December 1973. Article II, paragraph 2, expressly empowers the Rector of the University to conclude agreements safeguarding the academic freedom and autonomy of the University "in the name of the United Nations". On the other hand, Article XI, after specifying that the University is an autonomous organ, gives it, in paragraph 2, legal capacity and, in paragraph 3, the power to conclude agreements with governments, organizations and private parties. By contrast to Article II, the capacity and power under Article XI would seem to be exclusively those of the autonomous subsidiary body; whether they belong to the international sphere is not clear.

Nations therefore did not extend to it. In the second (*Jirjis* v. *U.N.R.W.A. Representative*, 1961), a Cairo court accepted that the Agency enjoyed the benefit of the Convention — as had, in the meantime, been expressly affirmed by the General Assembly in Resolution 1456(XIV) of 1959 — but reaffirmed that it possessed a separate juridical personality and was competent to enter into agreements on the international plane.[67] Another example concerns a subsidiary body of the International Labour Organization, the Centre for Advanced Technical and Vocational Training. A provision of the Statute of the Centre confers on it legal personality and such legal capacity as is necessary for the fulfilment of its purposes.[68] The intention was apparently essentially to enable the Centre to deal with private law matters in a manner which would limit the liability for obligations undertaken by it to its own funds and assets; its capacity to do so at its offices in Turin was ensured under an agreement between the I.L.O. and Italy. Nevertheless, when the Centre in 1972 wished to open an office in London the Protocol Department of the Foreign and Commonwealth Office took — and maintained — the view that the provision gave the Centre an international legal personality distinct from that of the International Labour Organization and that, accordingly, it could not rely on the Convention on the Privileges and Immunities of the Specialized Agencies.[69]

Perhaps examples such as the foregoing are primarily the expression of a sentiment that, in establishing subsidiary bodies, international organizations may be having their cake and eating it too. On the one hand, such bodies may have extensive autonomy and relieve the parent organization of responsibility for their actions; on the other, for such purposes as privileges and immunities,[70] or coverage by the Second Protocol to the Universal Copyright Convention,[71] they seek to have the benefit of belonging to the

[67] The cases are referred to in W. Dale, "U.N.R.W.A. — A Subsidiary Organ of the United Nations", 23 *I.C.L.Q.* 576, 591 (1974).

[68] Centre for Advanced Technical and Vocational Training, Art. VIII, para. 1.

[69] Letters of 15 March 1972 and 2 November 1973.

[70] It is now standard practice, as regards U.N. subsidiary organs, for coverage by the Convention on the Privileges and Immunities of the United Nations to be expressly affirmed. This may imply practical problems where the Secretary-General lacks direct disciplinary authority over the staff of a subsidiary body.

[71] This applies only to the U.N. family of organizations.

parent organization. At the same time, the apparent readiness to consider that bodies established by an organ of an international organization[72] and frequently having no "membership" can be independent persons in international law, opens new vistas. It may well be that the considerable problems which have been created in national law by the growth of groups of companies are being paralleled, in the sphere of international law, by the hiving off of certain functions of international organizations to subsidiaries.

(B) INTER-ORGANIZATION RELATIONS

Inter-State relations are based on the principle of respect for the independence and sovereignty of each State. Some comparable principle may be needed in inter-organization relations. What is at issue here is not the co-ordination of their activities which may overlap but the protection of their legal structures and institutions. A few examples may serve to illustrate the nature of the problem.

A number of organizations are empowered to set standards in their field of specialization. The manner in which they do so, and the obligations of Member States in relation to standards so set, are in many of these cases laid down in the constitution of the organization concerned. Where the standards take the form of international conventions, ratification then may create obligations, not only as between ratifying States, but also in relation to the organization.[73] Certain legal consequences flow from this position. For instance, the I.L.O., where the matter is of particular importance because employers and workers as well as governments have a role in the adoption and in the implementation of international labour conventions, submitted to the Vienna Conference on the Law of Treaties that one of the rules of the Organization, diverging from the general law of treaties, was that an inter-se agreement between States varying the terms of ratified international labour conventions was not permissible.[74] What then of standards adopted in other international organizations?

[72] The organ may be a limited one. The aforementioned I.L.O. Centre was set up by the Governing Body and not the General Conference.

[73] See below, Chapter III.

[74] See also M.H. Mendelson, "Reservations to the Constitutions of International Organizations", 45 *B.Y.* 137 (1971), who takes the view that inter-se variations

The question arose in 1978 with the adoption, under the auspices of I.M.C.O., of a Convention on Standards of Training, Certification and Watchkeeping for Seafarers. Article V of the Convention was drafted to provide that all prior treaties and conventions relating to standards of training, certification and watchkeeping for seafarers which were in force between parties to the new Convention would continue to have effect in respect of seafarers to whom the new Convention did not apply and matters for which it had not expressly provided. Concern was expressed by a tripartite I.L.O. delegation to the I.M.C.O. Conference seeing that there were I.L.O. Conventions which were applicable to seafarers to whom the new Convention applied and which dealt with matters provided for therein. This did not lead to a modification of the provision since the Conference declared itself satisfied that there was no conflict between the new and prior Conventions. The question of principle, namely whether the adoption of a convention elsewhere could in itself deprive I.L.O. standards of their effect, remained. It was considered in the I.L.O. Governing Body in November 1978. While some government members took the view that no body other than the International Labour Conference could amend international labour standards or deprive them of effect, others were uncertain of the respective authority of the Conference and of plenipotentiary conferences in a different framework.[75] Finally, the Governing Body was content to note that in this case the new Convention did not impair the effect of I.L.O. standards.[76]

Similar problems are posed by the Convention on the Elimination of All Forms of Discrimination against Women, adopted by the U.N. General Assembly in December 1979. As submitted by the Commission on the Status of Women, the draft convention provided that it would not affect existing conventions adopted under the auspices of the specialized agencies (only) to the extent that they provided for more extensive rights for women. Both I.L.O. and U.N.E.S.C.O. submitted memoranda on the subject.[77] After lengthy discussion, the General Assembly adopted a

are not possible in relation either to organizational or to regulatory standards (*ibid.*, at 145-6).

75 Doc. G.B. 208/14/25, paras. 13-16.

76 Minutes of the 208th Session of the Governing Body, IX/7.

77 U.N. Docs. E/5938 and A/32/218. Both organizations had adopted Conventions on matters dealt with in the U.N. text.

provision which was believed to be a compromise but in fact continues to pose the issue. Article 23 of the Convention provides that "[n]othing in this Convention shall affect any provisions that are more conducive to the achievement of equality between men and women which may be contained ... in any other international convention, treaty or agreement in force for [a State Party]". In this case, the practical consequences of the provision are unforeseeable.

Another legal problem of inter-organization relations, of importance within the United Nations family of organizations, is that of harmonizing United Nations — and particularly General Assembly — positions[78] on certain political issues with the constitutional law of specialized agencies.

One example relates to United Nations "invitations" that all assistance be denied to certain countries — in the 1960s Portugal, over a longer period South Africa. In 1967, there was lengthy correspondence between the United Nations and the International Bank for Reconstruction and Development, after the General Assembly requested the Secretary-General to consult with the Bank "in order to obtain compliance" with such resolutions.[79] A memorandum of the U.N. Legal Counsel analysed the Bank's Articles of Agreement and concluded that a "reasonable" interpretation of their terms permitted compliance with the resolutions. A memorandum of the General Counsel of the Bank contested the interpretation, while pointing out that competence to decide questions of interpretation lay with the Executive Directors of the Bank. The two memoranda also reflect conflicting views of the position of specialized agencies: the U.N. Legal Counsel found it "incongruous" that loans be granted by a U.N. family organization to countries the international conduct of which had been condemned virtually unanimously through the United Nations; the General Counsel of the Bank considered this to be "no more than

[78] We are not dealing here with mandatory sanctions in respect of which Members of the United Nations are required by the Charter to take action *inter alia* in other international agencies of which they are Members. However, even this can raise difficulties in other organizations. See, e.g., for an examination of the relevant provisions of the law of the European Communities, P.J. Kuyper, "Sanctions against Rhodesia: the E.E.C. and the Implementation of General Legal Rules", 12 *C.M.L.R.* 231 (1975).

[79] U.N Doc. A/6825, submitted under agenda items 35 and 66.

a reflection of the technical and functional character of the Bank" the Members of which had not deemed it appropriate to give it a larger function in the international community. Finally, the Executive Directors by a majority endorsed the position of the Bank's General Counsel.[80]

Some specialized agencies have similarly found it difficult to give effect to General Assembly resolutions calling on them to grant full membership to Namibia. For instance, when the International Labour Conference considered an application of the U.N. Council for Namibia for membership in the I.L.O., in June 1978, the Legal Adviser concluded that Namibia could not be admitted, for two main reasons: membership under the Constitution was open to States and Namibia had not yet attained statehood within the meaning given to the term in international law; and the Constitution placed obligations on Members of the Organization which could be satisfied only by independent States.[81] In reply the representatives of the Council for Namibia submitted a working paper in which the I.L.O. Constitution was interpreted to imply that in any question concerning the admission of new Members, the I.L.O. must take into consideration and follow the decisions of the United Nations.[82] An author favourable to the admission of Namibia has commented that "this position ... would seem to subject the I.L.O. to decisions taken by another organization, the U.N., even to the extent of overriding the I.L.O.'s own Constitution".[83] Namibia was finally admitted under a compromise

[80] At about the same time I.C.A.O. found that the provision of G.A. Res. 2107(XX) calling on States to deny Portuguese aircraft landing facilities was contrary to the Chicago Convention. For a more recent controversy concerning an I.M.F. loan to South Africa see G.A. Res. 37/2 and 37/32 and Doc. A/37/607.

[81] Record of Proceedings of the 64th Session of the International Labour Conference, 24/20-22.

[82] *Ibid.*, 24/23. All that the Constitution provides is that Member States of the United Nations may become Members of the I.L.O. by accepting the obligations of its Constitution. Another, somewhat absurd, example of "interpretation" of I.L.O. constitutional provisions on membership is provided by the indication in the *United Nations Yearbook*, during a period of years when the People's Republic of China did not actively participate in the work of the I.L.O., that China was not a Member of the I.L.O., with a footnote specifying that the I.L.O. considered it to be a Member.

[83] R. Zacklin, "The Problem of Namibia in International Law", 171 *R.C.A.D.I.*, 1981-II, p. 224 at 317. See also E. Osieke, "Admission for Membership in International Organizations: the Case of Namibia", 51 *B.Y.* 189 (1980), who

which is a masterpiece of legal fiction: the Conference considered that compliance with the terms of the Constitution was prevented only by the illegal occupation of Namibia, and affirmed that the rights of the Namibian people could not be frustrated by illegal actions.[84]

Questions of inter-organization relations of rather a different nature and of greater complexity are posed by the assumption, by the European Communities, of the external relations functions of their Members in matters falling within Community competence. Where these Members participate in other international organizations, their ability to give effect to their rights and obligations in such organizations may be affected. The literature on the subject[85] and some relevant decisions of the Court of Justice of the Communities[86] have addressed the matter primarily from the point of view of the internal law of the Communities. However, here also there may be a need for harmonizing the requirements of two legal orders.[87] Efforts with a view to such harmonization have been

points out that, under its Agreement with the United Nations, the obligations of the I.L.O. are limited to the submission of formal recommendations of the General Assembly to the competent I.L.O. organ.

[84] At the end of 1982, following decisions to admit Namibia by the organs of the I.A.E.A., the United States, as depositary Government of the Statute of the Agency, held the Instrument of Acceptance submitted by the Council for Namibia in abeyance pending comments by the Parties to the Statute, on the ground that the Statute did not permit membership in the Agency by an entity other than a State.

[85] See, e.g., P. Pescatore, "External Relations in the Case-law of the Court of Justice of the European Communities", 16 *C.M.L.R.* 615 at 628ff (1979); J.P. Jacqué, "La Participation de la C.E.E. aux Organisations Internationales Universelles", 21 *Ann. Français* 1975, p. 924; Kovar, see p. 14, note 38 above, at p. 903; "La condition internationale de la Communauté", *Cahiers de droit européen* 1978, notes, 5-6, at pp. 548ff.

[86] In particular, *Kramer and Others* (Joined cases 3, 4, 6/76) [1976] *E.C.R.* 1279 (decisions in the North East Atlantic Fisheries Commission); *Opinion of the Court Given Pursuant to Article* 228(1) *of the E.E.C. Treaty of 11 November* 1975 (Case 1/75) [1975] *E.C.R.* 1355 (decisions of the O.E.C.D.); *Draft Agreement Establishing a European Laying-up Fund for Inland Waterway Vessels* (Case 1/76) [1977] *E.C.R.* 741; *Re the Draft Convention on the Physical Protection of Nuclear Materials, Facilities and Transport* (Opinion 1/78) [1979] 1 *C.M.L. Reports* 131 (draft Convention elaborated in I.A.E.A.).

[87] See also the comment of K.R. Simmonds, "The Evolution of the External Relations Law of the European Economic Community", 28 *I.C.L.Q.* 644 at 664-5 (1979), as regards the application and interpretation of international agreements: "The principle of 'effectiveness', on which the Court has placed such weight, must in such a process of interpretation relate to the positions of

made, in particular by the Communities and the I.L.O.[88] The main problems concern international labour conventions and the application of the provisions of the I.L.O. Constitution relating thereto. For instance, under the Constitution, Member States of the I.L.O. are required to submit newly adopted Conventions to the authority competent to legislate or otherwise implement the instrument. It has been accepted that where a Community organ has the power to legislate on the subject-matter of a particular Convention, submission to that organ may satisfy the constitutional obligation, but a number of ancillary problems remain: should there be submission to national parliaments as well;[89] how can Member States ensure that, as expected under I.L.O. constitutional practice, submission is accompanied or rapidly followed by a statement as to the action to be taken; how can national employers' and workers' organizations be consulted on and advised of proposals for action? Again, because so many relevant requirements derive directly from the Constitution, ratification of international labour Conventions is open only to Member States of the I.L.O. Where, under Community law, the European Economic Community as such has the power to conclude treaties on a particular subject, there would have to be some form of delegation: either the Member States might advise the I.L.O. that they, as Members, will be bound by a ratification communicated by the Community, or the competent organ of the Community might delegate its power to ratify to the Member States. The choice is one of Community law and has not yet been made; the problem is particularly difficult in cases of "mixed competence". An even more difficult question is whether there would be consistency with obligations in relation to the I.L.O. if individual Member States were debarred from ratifying Conventions whenever one or more other Members of the Communities were unable or unwilling to comply with their standards. Finally, there are liable to be problems concerning the

all the parties to the agreement and not only to the effectiveness of the agreement *vis-à-vis* the Community's own policy of integration." (*Ibid.*, at 665.)

88 For I.L.O. Governing Body consideration, in 1981, of potential problem areas and relevant I.L.O. rules, see Doc. G.B. 215/SC/4/1 and G.B. 215/12/22. For early proposals put forward by the Commission of the Communities in 1980 see COM (80) 315 final.

89 For the second purpose of submission of informing the public. The United Kingdom has so submitted.

answerability of individual Member States for non-compliance with a ratified Convention where such non-compliance results from Community legislation. On all these issues each organization needs to avoid seeking to give "priority" to its law. Both need to bear in mind the importance of not allowing procedural difficulties to prejudice the effect of the substantive work of either.

3. Means of Applying International Law to International Organizations

There is no reason why rules of international law which are generally recognized as applicable between States and which are not by their nature unsuitable for international organizations should not be automatically binding on the latter.[90] Such a conclusion has been justified on the ground that States bound by rules of international law should not be able to evade them collectively. Alternatively, if international organizations are seen as legal entities distinct from their Members; the applicability of the relevant rules can be explained as a necessary implication of legal capacity and activity in the international legal order.[91] However that may be, it does not appear to have been suggested by any organization that it is free to accept or not to accept legal rules meeting the double test.

A rather different question is that of the relationship between international law and the internal law of organizations. It bears some similarity to the question of the relationship between international law and municipal law, and has been examined by reference to analogous concepts in relation to the European Communities, the internal law of which bears much greater resemblance to the legal order of a State than that of any other international organization.[92] However, as in the case of certain aspects of the law of treaties discussed earlier, the fact that a key element of

[90] H.G. Schermers takes it for granted that international organizations are bound by "general international law" (Schermers, see p. 3, note 1 above, at p. 1383).

[91] For an examination of the theoretical basis of the applicability of general international law, see A. Bleckmann, "Zur Verbindlichkeit des allgemeinen Völkerrechts für internationale Organisationen", *Zeitschrift für ausländisches öffentliches Recht und Völkerrecht* (1977), p. 107.

[92] See, e.g., K.M. Meessen, "The Application of Rules of Public International Law within Community Law", 13 *C.M.L.R.* 485 (1976); Kuyper, see p. 28, note 78 above; H.G. Schermers, "Community Law and International Law", 12 *C.M.L.R.* 77 (1975); G. Bebr, "Agreements concluded by the Community and their Possible Direct Effect", 20 *C.M.L.R.* 35 (1983). Earlier literature regarding

the internal law of most organizations is itself an international treaty may call for a different hierarchy of legal norms, and possibly a distinction between the priority given to *ius cogens* and to other rules of international law. Even as regards the Communities such questions have not yet been fully explored in practice.[93]

At the same time if, as has been suggested above, it is not certain to what extent, and with what possible modifications, rules of international law generally recognized as applicable between States may be suitable for international organizations, the most important issue is how a statement of appropriate rules, whether intended to be declaratory of existing law or to represent its progressive development, or both, may be given effect in relation to international organizations.

International organizations appear to be reluctant to admit that they can be bound by a treaty to the terms of which they have not, in one form or another, given their consent. The Court of Justice of the European Communities has been prepared to accept as "guidelines" or "general principles of law" international treaties in which the Member States, but not the Communities, have participated;[94] this is, of course, much easier in an organization with ten Members than in one with 150 or more. The Secretary-General of the United Nations, in performing depositary functions, has had to face the fact that, as regards the treatment of reservations, the terms of the Vienna Convention on the Law of Treaties do not correspond fully to decisions on the subject taken by the General Assembly in 1952 and 1957: in 1975 and again in 1976 he made it clear that he did not believe himself to have the authority to adjust his practice to the Vienna Convention in the absence of new

treaties is discussed in H.J. Geiser, *Les effets des accord conclus par les organisations internationales* (1977), pp. 117-29.

93 See Meessen (above, note 92) who takes the view that the treaties forming the basis of Community Law would prevail both over treaties and over general international law, but would be so interpreted as not to violate obligations thereunder.

94 *Nold, Kohlen-und Baustoffgrosshandlung* v. *Commission of the European Communities* (Case 4/73) [1974] *E.C.R.* 491; 55 *I.L.R.* 459, regarding human rights treaties; *Rutili* v. *Minister for the Interior* (Case 36/75) [1975] *E.C.R.* 1219; 62 *I.L.R.* 390, regarding human rights treaties; *Defrenne* v. *Société Anonyme Belge de Navigation Aérienne Sabena* (Case 43/75) [1976] *E.C.R.* 455, regarding I.L.O. Equal Remuneration Convention.

instructions from the General Assembly.[95] Similarly, while the I.L.O. has felt at least morally bound in its staff practices to take account of international labour standards adopted by the Organization and widely ratified by Member States, other organizations have often taken the view that these standards are not binding on organizations. Thus a U.N. legal opinion of 1973, concerning the legal status of a trade union seeking to represent U.N. staff in Geneva, stated that the Freedom of Association and Protection of the Right to Organize Convention, 1948 (ratified by nearly two-thirds of the membership of the Organization)

> is of course only applicable to those States that ratified it and not to any inter-governmental organizations they may belong to. If States feel obliged to bring the provisions or the principles of such treaties to bear on an international organization, they can do so by means of appropriate resolutions in the organization.[96]

In its statement on the draft articles on treaties between States and international organizations, submitted to the General Assembly in October 1983, the Administrative Committee on Co-ordination affirmed that it was essential "that no international organization be bound without its explicit consent by a convention incorporating the draft articles".[97]

Conversely, a number of States are reluctant to accept the participation of international organizations as parties on an equal footing with States in "law-making" multilateral conventions. Their argument of principle is that only States, as the original subjects of international law, are in a position in every respect to establish international law; organizations possess such capacity only in their respective fields of activity and within limits established by their rules.[98] Such participation would in any case raise some practical difficulties. One relates to the great number of international organizations: if the subject matter is of general concern would all be able

[95] *U.N.J.Y.B.* 1975, p. 204; *U.N.J.Y.B.* 1976, p. 210. The fact that the Vienna Convention was not yet in force does not appear to have been determining.

[96] *U.N.J.Y.B.* 1973, p. 171. The same opinion considered the right of association to be applicable to the United Nations by virtue of the Universal Declaration of Human Rights.

[97] U.N. Doc. A/C.6/38/4.

[98] See, e.g., U.N. Doc. A/38/145, p. 8. And note how Annex IX of the U.N. Convention on the Law of the Sea circumscribes the possible accession of an international organization.

to participate or only some;[99] and, if the latter, what would be the value, if any, of the convention in relation to those not participating? Another is that in this context the likelihood of controversy over the treaty-making capacity of particular organizations is greater than in that of bilateral or even multilateral arrangements in pursuance of their normal activities. Also, to what extent and in what manner would acceptance of the convention by international organizations be taken into account for the purpose of its entry into force? Finally, the diversity of practice of international organizations is liable to raise in acute form the problem of reservations to "codifying" treaties.

What then are the possible alternatives?

One possible approach is that of some Conventions on Privileges and Immunities. The United Nations Convention was "adopted", and that applicable to the specialized agencies "accepted" by the representative organs of the organization, prior to being opened to ratification or accession by States.[100] They speak expressly of being "in force" as between the organizations and ratifying or acceding States, and there is no doubt that the organizations consider themselves to be bound by their terms, without being parties thereto in the same sense as States. However, again, the great number of international organizations makes it more difficult to envisage this procedure in respect of a subject which is of interest to all of them, and the problem of "reservations" remains.[101]

Another possibility is a "third party" approach: the convention would be open to ratification and accession by States only but, on the assumption that it would create both rights and obligations for international organizations, these would be invited to consent thereto. This is essentially the approach of the Convention on the

99 At present there is a group of "principal international organizations" which are invited to send observers to codification conferences and which have been consulted on the draft articles concerning treaties between States and international organizations. They include the United Nations, the specialized agencies and the main regional organizations.

100 U.N. Doc. A/940 of September 1949 makes it clear that "acceptance" by a specialized agency was a condition precedent to accession in respect to that agency.

101 In the Convention on the Privileges and Immunities of the Specialized Agencies the Annexes for each organization in fact serve to take account of their differences.

Representation of States in their relations with International Organizations of a Universal Character: while Articles 86-9 make signature, ratification and accession a matter for States, Article 90 provides that "[a]fter the entry into force of the present Convention, the competent organ of an international organization of a universal character may adopt a decision to implement the relevant provisions of the Convention"; furthermore, under Article 2, the Convention only applies to representation in relation to a particular organization "when it has been accepted by the host State and the organization has completed the procedure envisaged by Article 90". The Convention may be a bad precedent in that it has not so far attracted the ratifications of host States and it may be both difficult and pointless for an organization to set in motion the Article 90 procedure unless there is some assurance of concurrent action by the host State. In any case it again applies only to a limited number of organizations and its approach cannot as readily be transposed to a convention concerning all organizations.[102]

In view of considerations such as the foregoing, the Administrative Committee on Co-ordination, in its submissions to the General Assembly in 1982 and 1983 on the subject of treaties between States and international organizations, explored a "soft law" alternative, namely the adoption of the draft articles by, and with the authority of, the United Nations not as a convention but as

> a standard of reference for action destined to harden into customary law. As regards the organizations of the United Nations system — that is, the major universal organizations — such adoption could be accompanied by a formal recommendation, which would be required, under the various relationship agreements, to be submitted to the competent organs of each organization ... As regards other organizations, it would be the

[102] See also "The Agreement on the Rescue of Astronauts, the Return of Astronauts and the Return of Objects Launched into Space", (G.A. Res. 2345 (XXII), Annex), the "Convention on International Liability for Damage Caused by Space Objects" (G.A. Res. 2777(XXVI), Annex), and "The Agreement Governing the Activities of States on the Moon and other Celestial Bodies" (*U.N.J.Y.B.* 1979, p. 109) which may apply to organizations responsible for conducting space activities, on the double condition that they declare their acceptance of the rights and obligations provided for in the instrument and that a majority of their Member States are parties to the instrument as well as to the Treaty on Principles Governing the Activities of States in the Exploration and Use of Outer Space.

responsibility of States Members both of the United Nations and of those organizations to take the necessary steps so that due account is taken of the standard of reference ...[103]

An analogous suggestion had already been submitted in comments on the first draft of the articles; however, the International Law Commission preferred to recommend that the draft articles be given the form of a general convention.[104] This was also the decision of the General Assembly, in 1982, in Resolution 37/112. As of now, that decision stands but all its practical implications remain to be decided.

B. Private International Law

Most international organizations differ from States in that their own legal order does not include rules regarding private law transactions.[105] A problem of choice of law accordingly arises for all such transactions of the organization. Moreover, the organization may be called upon to deal with legal situations in respect of which there exists a conflict of laws, without being able to draw upon rules reflecting a public policy of its own.

1. Transactions of the Organization

The determination of the proper law to govern various transactions of international organizations is a large subject on which there exists substantial literature.[106] Recently, a comprehensive review of doctrine and practice regarding the contracts concluded by international organizations with private persons — by far the largest segment of their private law transactions — was undertaken by the

103 U.N. Docs. A/C.6/37/L.12 and A/C.6/38/4.

104 Report of the International Law Commission on the Work of its 34th Session, General Assembly, Official Records, 37th Session, Supplement No. 10 (A/37/10), paras. 56-61.

105 Contracts of employment of international officials, generally accepted as being a matter for the internal law of organizations, are here left out of consideration.

106 Amongst the classics, see in particular C.W. Jenks (see p. 3, note 1 above); and F. Seyersted, "Applicable Law in Relations between Intergovermental Organizations and Private Parties", 122 *R.C.A.D.I.* 1967-III, p. 427.

Institute of International Law.[107] It is accordingly not proposed here to go over the same ground. Suffice it to say that the Institute survey found that there were no clear trends in practice and that, doctrinally, any answer to the question of the law applicable to the contracts of international organizations could not be divorced from wider controversies concerning such issues as the possible "internationalization" of certain private law transactions, the conclusion of contracts *sans loi*, and the choice of law by international (arbitral) tribunals.

There are, nevertheless, a number of issues of particular relevance to international organizations.

The first relates to the connection, if any, between immunity from jurisdiction and applicable law.[108] In principle,[109] international organizations enjoy immunity everywhere. Moreover, as indicated earlier, for many of them[110] that immunity has been wider than that of States may be because no distinction has been made between acts *iure imperii* and acts *iure gestionis*. This means that States are not in a position to enforce their law against an international organization. But does it also mean that no municipal law can apply to international organizations unless it has been expressly chosen or incorporated by them? The arguments for immunity from jurisdiction — in particular the need to protect organizations from abusive, restrictive and divergent decisions of courts of different countries — do not justify the inapplicability of municipal law. Texts on immunities do not specify such inapplicability. On the other hand, some organizations firmly believe in the inapplicability of municipal law, at least in relation to contracts.[111] For instance, "in no case does the United Nations consider the law of any national system to be binding upon it either in the execution of contracts or in dispute settlements arising therefrom", while

[107] *Annuaire de l'Institut de droit international*, Vol. 57, 1 (1977), pp. 1-191 (Preparatory and final reports, by N. Valticos), *ibid.*, II, pp. 264-317 (discussion); 332-7 (resolution).

[108] Where there is no immunity, jurisdiction, including the freedom of the parties to resort to arbitration, may also be affected.

[109] For organizations with limited membership this may be dependent, as regards transactions having a connection with non-Member States, on the recognition of immunity under general rules of international law.

[110] *I.e.*, for those whose immunity from jurisdiction is not expressly limited by reference to the nature of their activities.

[111] The applicability of the *lex situs* to immovable property is generally accepted.

apparently accepting "from a practical point of view" to give attention to ensuring that contracts are in general compliance with the law of the place of conclusion, the law of the place of performance, and the national law of the private parties with which the contract is concluded.[112] The Rapporteur of the Institute took a more pragmatic stand: "On ne saurait ... exclure *a priori* qu'un droit étatique puisse être considéré comme régissant un contrat silencieux sur la loi applicable ..."[113] In other words, it is conceivable that an arbitral or administrative tribunal seized of a contract to which an international organization is a party and which does not specify the law to be applied might find a municipal system of law to be the proper law of the contract. When it would do so in practice may be related to the nature of the contract. To take two extreme examples, the application of municipal law is more likely to a contract for the purchase of pencils for the headquarters of the organization from a company in the same country than to an arrangement under which an organization subcontracts a part of the performance of its obligations under a technical co-operation agreement with a government. However, not all contracts can be as readily classified.

The question of the possible applicability of national legal systems may be of importance also in relation to imperative provisions claiming to override the proper law, whether expressly chosen or not. It is often assumed that international organizations are entirely free to choose the law applicable to their private law transactions. F. Seyersted[114] specifically asserted that all statutory restrictions on such freedom were barred by the immunity of the organizations. On the other hand, C.W. Jenks[115] considered that such restrictions were applicable, in principle, but believed them to be of little practical importance because organizations were expressly exempted from some (e.g. fiscal legislation) and because others had little relevance to the organizations' transactions. In the twenty

[112] *U.N.J.Y.B.* 1976, p. 164. A similar distinction between voluntary compliance and legal subjection is made by B. Knapp, "Questions juridiques relatives à la construction d'immeubles par les organisations internationales", 33 *Ann. Suisse* 1977, p. 51 at 69; while recognizing that compliance with rules relating to electricity and sewage is necessary in practice, he takes the view that these rules are not binding.

[113] Valticos, see p. 37, note 107 above, at 56.

[114] See p. 37, note 106 above, at pp. 468-70.

[115] See p. 3, note 1 above, at pp. 148-9.

years since he wrote legislative provisions regarded as imperative have mushroomed, and the practical importance of the matter may no longer be so negligible. For instance, restrictions on technology transfer may have relevance to purchases of an organization for technical co-operation.[116] Assuming that their applicability is not precluded as a matter of principle, there would be a choice of law problem: the imperative provisions of which legal system could claim to be applied. Traditionally, the mandatory law of the forum alone was applied to the detriment of the law applicable under normal conflict rules; where jurisdiction is given to international administrative or arbitral tribunals, there is no forum in the sense of that practice.[117] However, it is beginning to be accepted that the imperative provisions of the law which would be applicable in the absence of express choice may fall to be applied despite such choice, and that even those of a third State with an overriding interest may be given effect or at least taken into account (with a similar practical result).[118] It could even be argued that, while one national legal system owes little consideration to the public policy of another as reflected in imperative provisions, international organizations might be expected to respect the relevant concerns of their Member States. The subject merits further reflection.

Widely, it is the assumption of organizations that the application and interpretation of their contractual obligations will be decided by reference to "general principles of law", irrespective of whether this has been expressly specified or not. Such confidence may not be altogether justified.

[116] In relation to this particular example, reference must be made also to the exemption, commonly found in texts on immunities, of the property of organizations from export restrictions.

[117] For an examination of the practice of international arbitral tribunals regarding the applicability of imperative provisions of a national legal system see Yves Derain, "Les normes d'application immédiate dans la jurisprudence arbitrale international", *Le Droit des Relations Economiques Internationales* (1982). As regards international organizations the law of the country in which they are established appears sometimes to be regarded as the "forum".

[118] See, e.g., Article 7, paragraph 1, of the E.E.C. Convention on the Law Applicable to Contractual Obligations of June 1980. Similar trends may be found in the Austrian Federal Act of 1978 on private international law, in Swiss draft legislation presently before Parliament and in the U.S. Second Restatement of the Law, on conflicts of laws.

First, one reason for not making express provision in contracts for the applicability of general principles of law is that the other party may hesitate to agree.[119] Insofar as arbitral tribunals, in particular, will seek to determine the common intention of the parties, the road to the application of such principles — unless the parties subsequently agree on reference to them specifically for the point in dispute — may not be direct. Moreover, the situation regarding, on the one hand, contracts between States and private parties and, on the other, contracts between organizations and private parties, is very different. It is not uncommon to find recourse to general principles of law in or in respect of international contracts between States and private parties, and particularly investment contracts. They are intended to serve as a protection for the private party against the use by the State of its own legal order to the private party's detriment.[120] In contracts between international organizations and private parties the shoe is, as it were, on the other foot: it is the organizations which desire the recourse to general principles of law, not so much for the protection of their interests as to emphasize their distance from national legal systems. While, therefore, the status of the organizations may be an argument for the non-application of a national system of law, considerations of justice and equity will not weigh heavily in favour of such a course.

Second, there are many different ideas as to what is meant by recourse to "general principles of law". In contracts between States and private parties such recourse is often supplementary to the application of the national legal system(s) of one or both of the parties and consists in turning towards a wider and more representative range of such systems both to fill gaps and, occasionally, as a corrective. Since, in the case of international organizations, one of the aims is to underline their status as international persons it may well be that the sense given by them to the phrase is that of Article 38(1)(c) of the Statute of the International Court of Justice. Contracts would then in principle be made subject to public international law — always assuming that this is possible in relations with

[119] See, e.g., Seyersted, p. 37, note 106 above, at p. 506.

[120] See, e.g., P. Lagarde, "Approche critique de la Lex Mercatoria", *Le Droit des Relations Economiques Internationales* (1982), p. 132; A.A. Fatouros, "International Law and the Internationalized Contract", 74 *A.J.I.L.* 134 (1980); D.M. McRae, "Legal Obligations and International Organizations", 11 *Canadian Yearbook* 87 (1973).

private parties[121] — and international law, since it is poor in established relevant rules, would be supplemented by general principles drawn from municipal law.[122] More dubiously, particularly where the contracts in question do not relate to anything which could be regarded as falling under a *lex mercatoria*, the general principles of law drawn from municipal systems might be regarded as a distinct legal order. In any of these eventualities it is far from clear what "distillation" of municipal law may be regarded as a general principle of law. At the same time, the greater the extent to which general principles are relied upon the more relevant that question becomes. The Swiss Government has recently taken the view that a rule, even though uniformly laid down by different countries, must, in order to become a general principle of the law of nations, be applied "de manière particulièrement marquée au cours d'une longue période et avoir un caractère éminemment représentatif".[123] The principle would certainly have to be reasonably widely accepted; recent arbitrations have shown that on some important issues there is no convergence of major legal systems.[124] The main example of regular judicial recourse to general principles drawn from municipal law in the framework of an international organization — that of the Court of Justice of the European Communities[125] — is too atypical to serve as a guide; the Communities have a limited number of Members, with much

[121] For an affirmative view, see F.A. Mann, "The Proper Law of Contracts Concluded by International Persons", 35 *B.Y.* 34, 1959; J.A. Barberis, "Nouvelles Questions concernant la personnalité juridique internationale", 179 *R.C.A.D.I.* 1983-I, p. 145.

[122] A very clear exposition of the role of general principles as a supplementary source of law is given in P. Weil, "Principes généraux du droit et contrats d'Etat", *Le Droit des Relations Economiques Internationales* (1982), pp. 403-4.

[123] Message of the Federal Council to Parliament of 10/12/1979 (L. Caflisch, "La pratique Suisse en matiére de droit international public 1980", 37 *Ann. Suisse*, p. 139 at 184-5). The question at issue was whether the fact that all industrialized countries having legislation on the subject of limited civil liability in nuclear matters made such limitation a general principle of law. The test proposed parallels that of international custom. Barberis, see note 121 above, at p. 197, suggests that frequently so-called general principles of law are in fact custom.

[124] See, e.g., *B.P.* v. *Libya*, 53 *I.L.R.* 297.

[125] For an analysis on relevant case law (which does not necessarily or even primarily relate to contracts), see M. Akehurst, "The Application of General Principles of Law by the Court of Justice of the European Communities", 52 *B.Y.* 29 (1981).

common culture, and a legal order which is more akin to that of a State than that of any other international organization. Even there the extent to which principles known only to some Members can be used is an issue. Elsewhere experience is very limited.

All this is not to say that general principles of law should not be used as a source; great international lawyers have spoken of their role in legal progress.[126] However, some heed should be paid to warnings from other authoritative voices. Sir Robert Jennings has expressed his concern

> about the continuing tendency of some to regard Article 38(1)(c) as a blank cheque to go delving among selected municipal laws ... The large approach to general principles may even have brought about harm. It has encouraged people to argue from quite general principles, divorced from the rules that give them meaning: rules that qualify, that temper and restrict ...

Sir Hersch Lauterpacht, dealing with general principles of law in connection with judicial legislation,[127] advised caution and restraint for the protection of that still tender plant, international adjudication.

2. *Conflict Situations*

There are several subject areas in which an international organization may be faced with conflicting indications as to the rights of

[126] See, e.g., Lord McNair, "The General Principles of Law Recognized by Civilized Nations", 33 *B.Y.* 1 (1957).

[127] *The Development of International Law by the International Court* (1958), pp. 166, 172. Akehurst, see note 125 above, at p. 39, has found that link in the work of the Court of Justice of the European Communities:

> The Court can choose to give greater weight to the laws of some Member States than to the laws of others: it can, in certain circumstances, choose from among conflicting principles of national law those principles which it regards as best or most progressive; very often a principle has to be stated in very broad or abstract terms in order to transcend differences of detail between national legal systems, and the Court inevitably has a good deal of discretion in deciding how such vague principles should be applied to the facts of particular cases. In all these ways, the application of general principles of law by the Court is a creative process and not merely a mechanical process ... In short, there is a tendency for general principles, borrowed initially from the law of Member States, to evolve into principles of judge-made law. (*Ibid.*)

others which it must recognize in its own activities. For instance, questions of applicable law may arise where material protected by copyright is drawn upon in connection with the preparation and use of teaching materials for technical co-operation activities: are the rights of the author (and their limits, in relation to certain types of use) defined by the law of the country of publication of the original material, by the law of the country in which the organization has its headquarters or by the law of the country to which the technical co-operation is being given? In most cases practical problems can be avoided by following the rule most beneficial to the other party or most familiar to him (such as, in the case of copyright material, that of the country of publication). However, in one area no ready escape from conflict situations is possible, namely that of the personal status and family situation of staff members in relation to entitlement to various forms of family benefit and in particular to pensions.

What is primarily at issue is the recognition of divorces and of (second) marriages,[128] without any internal rules regarding such questions as jurisdiction in matters of divorce, the relevance of the fact that the country of origin of the staff member does not provide for divorce, or the conditions of validity of marriages in form and substance.

One possible approach is to be guided by the law of the country of origin of the staff member. This appears to be the policy of the United Nations. A memorandum of September 1979 states expressly that "[i]t is United Nations policy to determine the marital status for United Nations administrative purposes by reference to the law of the home country of the staff member concerned".[129] In that case the finding was that the divorce at issue was not valid under the law of the country where it had been obtained, and a

[128] In an article on "The Law Applicable to International Officials", 18 *I.C.L.Q.* 739 (1969) the present author suggested that other problems of family law, such as the recognition of adoptions, could be avoided by elaborating, in staff and pension rules, self-contained criteria for the entitlement in question, perhaps expressed in terms of dependency rather than in terms of legal relationship. This has been done by some organizations: see, for the interpretation and application of the relevant W.H.O. rule in *Watters* v. *W.H.O.*, I.L.O. Administrative Tribunal, Judgement No. 422, Forty-Fifth Ordinary Session, November 1980.

[129] *U.N.J.Y.B.* 1979, p. 182.

reference to the home country was thus hardly necessary. Similarly, a memorandum of January 1976[130] tested a Mexican divorce and remarriage against the staff member's "personal legal status" under the laws of his home country; at the same time, it found that they would not have been valid, not only under those laws but also under the laws of the matrimonial residence prior to the divorce, of the country of nationality of the two women concerned, of the place of the first marriage "and indeed in most jurisdictions".[131] Much more difficult questions arise where, say, the country of origin of the staff member does not provide for divorce but he is divorced and remarried in the country of his habitual residence.[132] Giving automatic priority to the law of the country of origin in such case may ignore facts recognized "in most jurisdictions" and produce hardship which cannot be justified entirely by the fact that, by retaining home leave and repatriation rights, the staff member does not officially sever his ties with his country of origin. Moreover, there are cases in which the position of the law of the country of origin is itself far from self-evident.

An alternative possibility is to accept any formal legal document issued by an authority competent for the purpose in the country of issue, or to do so at least unless or until the validity of such a document has been denied by the judgment of a court of the staff member's nationality or domicile, as the case may be. Such an approach — followed by a number of organizations — can be justified, on the one hand, by the respect owed by the organization to the legal institutions of all its Members and, on the other, by the lack of competence of the organization to review the acts of these institutions and their recognition, or otherwise, elsewhere. As an administrative arrangement, for such purposes as family allowances or travel, it probably corresponds to the current facts of the staff member's family situation and provides a practical solution. However, it would not seem to be a legal solution that could be applied by an administrative tribunal called upon to adjudicate on two conflicting claims to a pension; the priority it gives to the latest

130 *U.N.J.Y.B.* 1976, p. 239. 131 *Ibid.*, p. 240.

132 As early as 1929 Swiss courts decided that international officials could be considered to be domiciled in Switzerland for the purpose of divorce jurisdiction. See *Parlett* v. *Parlett*, 5 *Ann. Dig.* 316.

legal act may go to a system of law which has no reasonable connection with the staff member's personal status.

One question which arises is to what extent international treaties — which are not binding on the organizations or open to accession by them — can serve as guides for their action in the matter. There are now Hague Conventions both on the recognition of divorces (1970) and on the recognition of the validity of marriages (1978). They are not yet widely ratified and hence cannot yet be said to rally an international consensus or to represent general principles of conflict law; in these circumstances, is it open to an organization, as its own policy, to refuse to accept evidence of a divorce, for instance, on the ground that the conditions of Article 2 of the Convention on the recognition of divorces were not satisfied? Also, the texts in effect leave key issues open. For instance, Article 7 of the Convention on the recognition of divorces gives contracting States the possibility of refusing to recognize a divorce when, at the time it was obtained, both the parties were nationals of States which did not provide for divorce and of no other State; is it within the competence of an international organization to decide to refuse recognition in such a case? Since the action of the organization may affect persons which are in no direct relationship to it, it is not as free as it would be in a matter falling wholly within its internal law to draw upon other legal sources.

In effect, there is not at present any generally valid solution to problems of family law as seen from an international "forum". Recourse will accordingly be had to more or less satisfactory practical solutions. The most cynical — in that it gives everyone something and deprives everyone of something — is to use rules designed for polygamous marriages and regard as such anyone with a claim under some system of law to be a spouse. There may even be cases in which the result is socially justifiable.

2

Participation in International Organizations: Representation and Representativity

Any organization normally determines, by express rules or otherwise, the participants in its operation and the manner of their participation. The determination should be designed to further the aims and purposes of the organization and the effectiveness of its work. This means that, beyond the enumeration of the categories of participants which may be admitted, the basis of the contribution that can be made by each needs to be considered and the principles governing admission to participation refined accordingly.

In the case of international organizations the process of consideration and refinement is fraught with difficulties. As regards the participation of States and governments the issues are complicated by notions drawn from inter-State relations, such as those of recognition and sovereign equality, and decisions are greatly influenced by the political concerns of existing Member States. Accordingly, in the Survey of International Law prepared by the Secretary-General of the United Nations in 1971 for the International Law Commission's review of its long-term programme, the view was expressed that the issue of membership and representation in international organizations appeared "to raise doctrinal difficulties which might be difficult to solve, and to be dependent, as regards clarification and resolution, on a political process in which States are directly engaged".[1] As regards the participation of entities and persons other than States and goverments, legal rules have little to draw upon in traditional international law and remain, with few exceptions, rather crude.

[1] *Y.B.I.L.C.* 1971-II, Part Two, p. 80.

A. States and Governments

1. Membership

What are the minimum conditions for membership in an international organization in the absence of, or leaving out of account, specific provisions governing the matter? In an advisory opinion which is frequently forgotten, the Permanent Court of International Justice in 1930 addressed itself to that question.[2] The specific issue before the Court was whether the Free City of Danzig could become a Member of the International Labour Organization. The Constitution of the Organization as then in force (Part XIII of the Treaty of Versailles) contained no provision on the subject; indeed there was doubt whether entities which were not Members of the League of Nations could become Members of the Organization.[3] The problem raised by the Free City of Danzig was that its foreign relations were, in accordance with Article 104 of the Treaty of Versailles, conducted by Poland; the Court found that this meant, in practice, that the Polish Government could not impose its policy on the Free City against its will, but that the Free City could not call upon Poland to take steps regarding its foreign relations which were opposed to Poland's own policy. The Court considered that, in these circumstances, the Free City was not able to undertake such acts as ratifying international labour conventions or filing complaints against other Members. On the ground that there was no constitutional provision "which absolves a Member of the I.L.O. from complying with the obligations of membership or excuses it from participating in the normal activities of the Organization if it cannot first obtain the consent of some other Member of the Organization", the Court held that Danzig was not able to become a Member unless there were an agreement under which Poland undertook not to object to any action by Danzig as a Member of the I.L.O. President Anzilotti, in a powerful dissenting opinion, considered that the Court had set the test too high. Referring to the membership, in the League and the I.L.O., of certain dominions and self-governing colonies, he took the view that a candidate for

[2] *Free City of Danzig and International Labour Organisation, P.C.I.J.* Ser. B, no. 18 (1980), p. 1; 5 *Ann. Dig.* 410.

[3] The Court left that issue aside.

admission had to be able to comply with the obligations of membership — no more — and that such matters as ratifying conventions and filing complaints were not obligations.

Express provisions included in the constitution of various organizations since that time reflect the conditions which might be regarded as necessary to the effective functioning of the organization very imperfectly. For instance, while it is frequently specified that candidates for membership must accept the obligations of membership,[4] the requirement that they must also be able to give effect to these obligations is spelt out much more rarely.[5] Some organizations — e.g. the Council for Mutual Economic Assistance and the Council of Europe — expect a commitment to the aims and purposes of the organization (which others consider, perhaps, as being included in the acceptance of constitutional obligations). Participation in and furtherance of the work of the organization is rarely mentioned;[6] an interesting exception is the Hague Conference on Private International Law which opens membership to States "the participation of which is from a juridical point of view of importance for the work of the Conference".

The relative incompleteness of express provisions lends importance to the issue which came before the International Court of Justice in 1948,[7] namely, whether such provisions are exhaustive. The Opinion of the Court relates only to the United Nations. The extent to which its reasoning is of relevance to other organizations depends on the drafting of the pertinent provisions of their Constitutions. It would seem to be legitimate to consider that, whereas the organs of an organization the Constitution of which states membership to be "open" to entities meeting conditions specified in the Constitution or even provides for the

[4] One might think that this was merely an expression of the principle *Pacta Sunt Servanda.*

[5] Such a requirement is contained, for instance, in Art. 4 of the Statute of the Council of Europe and, of course, in Art. 4(1) of the Charter of the United Nations.

[6] The Statute of the Council of Europe provides for "sincere and effective collaboration".

[7] *Admission of a State to the United Nations, I.C.J. Reports* 1948, p. 57; 15 *Ann. Dig.* 333. The events which led to that Opinion and a second one two years later, and which shed little light on legal qualifications for membership, are not further considered here.

"entitlement" of such entities to membership,[8] may not be able to add to these conditions (while having some leeway in interpreting them), organizations given large discretion by the terms of their Constitution are not so restricted.[9]

There have certainly been cases in such organizations in which issues bearing on the capacity of certain entities to assume membership in an organization have been considered without reference to specific texts. Among significant examples are the admissions, in 1950-1951, of the Federal Republic of Germany, Japan and Vietnam to a number of specialized agencies.

The Federal Republic of Germany sought membership in F.A.O., I.L.O., U.N.E.S.C.O. and W.H.O. at a time when it was still formally under occupation and its external relations, in particular, were being handled by the Occupying Powers. Its request for admission was accompanied by a communication from the Allied High Commission for Germany affirming that the High Commission would not exercise any of the powers reserved to it under the Occupation Statute in such a way as to prevent or hinder the fulfilment by the Federal Republic of the obligations and responsibilities attaching to membership of the Organization. In the I.L.O. the Committee which examined the application for membership considered "on this clear understanding" that the applicant Government "has the international status necessary to enable it to discharge the obligations involved in membership of the Organization".[10] In the Economic and Social Council of the United Nations, called upon to give its *nihil obstat* to admission to U.N.E.S.C.O., the representative of the United Kingdom explained that full independence was not necessary for admission to a specialized agency; what was necessary was full independence in the sphere of action of the organization and a sufficient ability to assume the direction of external affairs in one's own name.[11] The opposition of the U.S.S.R. to the admission of the Federal Republic was based, not so much on its ability to act

[8] For instance in the Organization of African Unity.

[9] In the European Economic Community the conditions of admission are so complex that they are required by Article 23A of the Treaty of Rome to be the subject of an agreement between the Member States and the applicant State.

[10] Record of Proceedings of the 34th Session of the International Labour Conference (1951), pp. 505-6.

[11] 12th Session, 468th Sitting. For a critique of this view and a description of the admission of the Federal Republic of Germany, Japan, Austria and Italy to the

internationally, as on the fear that it might be taken to represent the German people as a whole. On the other hand, Czechoslovakia affirmed that only "independent and sovereign States" could be Members of an international organization.

The situation of Japan was analogous. Its application for membership was accompanied by a statement, on behalf of the Supreme Commander for the Allied Powers, that his authority, while unimpaired, would not be exercised in such a way as to hamper the Japanese Government in fulfilling its obligations of membership. In the I.L.O. admission was recommended to the Conference by the Selection Committee in terms which were identical to those used in the case of the Federal Republic.[12] In the Economic and Social Council the U.S.S.R. alleged that Japan was not capable of becoming a Member of an international organization, and that the Supreme Commander could not authorize it to do so, on the ground that the Allied Commission for the Far East had decided that Japan should not have responsibility in the field of foreign affairs. On the other hand, the United States explained that the policy of permitting Japan to accede to international agreements in technical fields was adopted in conformity with Allied decisions to further its economic and cultural advancement.

As regards Vietnam, the problem was that, although the French protectorate over Indochina had come to an end, there continued to be a "special relationship" under which France had some influence over Vietnam's foreign affairs. In the I.L.O., where the matter was considered in June 1950[13] (*I.e.* earlier than elsewhere), the case was dealt with as a parallel to that of Danzig. Acting on the lines suggested by the Permanent Court in that case, a French representative made a formal statement recognizing the rights and obligations of Vietnam as a Member of the I.L.O.: "This includes the right to ratify international labour conventions freely and, in general, to undertake, within the framework of the I.L.O., any action which Vietnam considers useful in furtherance of the aims of the Organization". By reference to this declaration the Committee

I.M.F., see J. Gold, *Membership and Non-Membership in the International Monetary Fund* (1974), pp. 71-89.

[12] See note 10 above, at pp. 508-10.

[13] Record of Proceedings of the 33rd Session of the International Labour Conference (1950), pp. 402-4.

examining the application for membership concluded that Vietnam had the international status necessary to enable it to discharge the obligations involved therein.

If, as the decisions on admission in these various cases imply, the test of suitability for membership is that of capacity to participate effectively in the work of the Organization, the reference, in constitutional provisions of international organizations, to membership[14] of "States" is a factor of confusion in that it seems to introduce a test drawn from general international law as developed in inter-State relations and not germane to the specific needs of the organization. There may be ambiguity in the use of the term. As has frequently been pointed out, the term "States" is found in Article 3 of the United Nations Charter (original Members) as well as in Article 4 (further admissions) and was included there in full knowledge of the fact that some of the original Members — India, Lebanon, Philippines, Syria (not to mention Byelorussia and Ukraine) — were not at the time fully sovereign States.[15] Contrariwise, the participation at the Bretton Woods Conference of some of these entities may have been one of the reasons for the use of the term "countries" instead of "States" in the I.M.F. Articles of Agreement.[16] Again, Article 156 of the U.N. Convention on the Law of the Sea provides that all "States" Parties are *ipso facto* Members of the International Sea-Bed Authority; Paragraph 3 of the Article suggests that, as used therein, the term covers the associated States and internally self-governing territories which may become parties to the Convention under Part XVII, although they are not covered by the term in that Part. However that may be, there is advantage in the use of terms such as "countries" (I.M.F., Bank) or "nations" (F.A.O.). For instance, whatever may have been the merits, in relation to the work of the organizations concerned, of the admission to membership of Namibia, there is no doubt that its legal

[14] We are not dealing here with devices such as associate membership or membership with qualified rights.

[15] See, e.g., H. Kelsen, *The Law of the United Nations* (1950), pp. 60-1, who nevertheless takes the view that under Article 4 only fully sovereign States may be admitted.

[16] See, Gold, p. 49, note 11 above, at pp. 43-51. Another reason apparently was the attendance of Danish and French participants who did not then represent a State, but whose participation would enable their "country" to be an original Member.

status created fewer difficulties in F.A.O. than in organizations providing for membership of "States".[17] A requirement of statehood makes recognition as a State of an entity seeking membership by a substantial number of existing Members of some legal relevance, even though such recognition may have been given or withheld for reasons of no concern to the organization. It is also likely that the reticence of existing Members in relation to the admission of entities not yet recognized by them is at least in part related to the fear that such admission constitutes an affirmation of the "statehood" of the entity in question.[18] The opposition for many years, even in the specialized agencies, to the admission of the German Democratic Republic was an example of this.[19] Use of the term may be one manifestation of the notion that international organizations are necessarily created by and composed of States which, it has been suggested in Chapter I, may be too rigid in concept. To the legal order of individual organizations, as to the sphere of international law in general, it is possible to apply the doctrine developed by the International Court of Justice in the *Reparation for Injuries Suffered in the Service of the United Nations* case: "The subjects of law in any legal system are not necessarily

[17] It should be noted that, in the I.L.O., the Office legal opinion which concluded that the admission of Namibia would not be in conformity with the Constitution, discussed the nature of "Statehood" within the meaning of the Constitution by reference to capacity to give effect to constitutional obligations, in the light of the *Danzig* Opinion. At the same time, it expressed the view that the terms of the Constitution clearly and deliberately excluded membership by an international authority responsible for administration of a territory (*i.e.* the Council for Namibia).

[18] For a view that admission establishes a rebuttable presumption that the international organization has correctly evaluated the elements of Statehood, see a Note of 7 February 1974 of the Direction du droit international public of the Swiss Federal Political Department, L. Caflisch, "La pratique Suisse en matière de droit international public" 1974, 31 *Ann. Suisse* 1975, 155, 210-13. As early as 1948 O. Schachter suggested that organizations might make it clear that their action did not imply recognition by Member States, "The Development of International Law through the Legal Opinions of the United Nations Secretariat", 25 *B.Y.* 91 at 114-15 (1948).

[19] See, e.g., Official Records of W.H.O., No. 169, 21st World Health Assembly, 1968, Part II, at p. 73, for the statement by the British delegate: "The Constitution makes it clear that membership of the W.H.O. is open only to States. If the Assembly approves this application, its decision would involve recognition of the Soviet Zone of Germany as a State."

identical ... and their nature depends on the needs of the community."[20]

Looking at organizations as communities with their own legal principles and needs also prompts the question whether there is room for "non-recognition" by the organization (as opposed to the reflection, in certain decisions of the organization, of the policies of non-recognition of individual Member States). The question is distinct from that of whether an international organization (and in particular the United Nations) can require its Members not to recognize certain entities as the United Nations has sought to do in relation to Rhodesia, the Bantustans and the Turkish Republic of Cyprus. It may be of more practical relevance to representation of Members, to be considered below, than to admission. Nevertheless, there is room for the view that a doctrine akin to non-recognition has, potentially, a double role. First, it may be appropriate for organizations, as for States, to refuse to recognize the consequences of the violation of certain principles of the international community such as the prohibition of intervention by force or the right to self-determination.[21] Second, there may be the right of organizations — as a parallel to certain conditions made by States for "recognition" in the establishment of bilateral relations — to require candidates for admission to have characteristics which correspond to the aims and purposes of the organization.[22] The latter aspect merges with

[20] *I.C.J. Reports* 1949, p. 174, 178; 16 *Ann. Dig.* 318, 321

[21] H.M. Blix, "Contemporary Aspects of Recognition", 130 *R.C.A.C.I.*, 1970-II, p. 587 cites the position, in 1933, of a special advisory committee of the League regarding the admission of Manchuko to the U.P.U. and the deletion, in 1965, of the signature by Rhodesia of the Final Act of the Plenipotentiary Conference of I.T.U. G. Fischer "La non-reconnaissance du Transkei", 22 *Ann. Français*, 1976, p. 63 considers that what is at issue is not the irregular origin of a State but the fact that its very existence violates a rule of law. The decision of the International Labour Conference to assimilate Namibia to a State for the purpose of Membership on the ground that only South Africa's illegal occupation prevented it from achieving Statehood is a different form of non-recognition.

[22] For instance, candidates for admission to the I.L.O. are generally expected to confirm that it is their policy to respect freedom of association, although such respect is an aim of the Organization and not an obligation under its Constitution. As indicated above, in some organizations (e.g. Council of Europe) respect for certain principles is expressly required. The provision of the U.N. Charter that a candidate for admission must be "peace-loving" falls into the same category.

the general issue of conditions for membership. It may have relevance also to termination of membership.

It is debatable, and debated, whether expulsion or other exclusion from participation in an organization of a Member who violates the obligations or disregards the basic principles of its Constitution furthers the aims and purposes of the organization. One of the main arguments of those who oppose such sanctions is that by excluding a Member, and releasing it from the obligations of membership, all leverage on the recalcitrant State is lost. Quite a number of organizations do not make constitutional provision for expulsion and the better view appears to be that there is no power to expel in the absence of express provision.[23] It may well be, however, that there is a difference, as regards the purpose and effect of expulsion, between universal organizations and some with more limited membership.[24] As regards the former, there is force in C.W. Jenks' formulation:

> The universality and permanence of the world community preclude recourse to expulsion as an effective sanction for violation of its standards; such problems must be solved within its membership by insistence on the obligations of membership, not by measures of expulsion or exclusion the practical effect of which is to release the offender from these obligations. The world community is not a club of the mutually congenial but an experiment in the organized government of all mankind.[25]

On the other hand, the work of a variety of smaller organizations is predicated at least in part upon a convergence of interests and

[23] For instance, it was agreed in the I.L.O. in 1963 that a constitutional amendment making express provision for expulsion was necessary. Such an amendment, adopted in 1964, has not obtained the number of ratifications necessary to bring it into force. In 1979 a number of Western Countries took the view that the expulsion of South Africa by the U.P.U. in the absence of express provision was unlawful.

[24] T. Oppermann, *Berichte der Deutschen Gesellschaft fur Völkerrecht*, vol. 17 (1975), distinguishes, as regards expulsion, between "necessary" and "optional" organizations.

[25] *Universality and Ideology in the I.L.O.* (1969), p. 7. It is significant that the conflict between the concepts of world community, on the one hand, and "club", on the other, became apparent even in the discussions regarding the forced withdrawal of Czechoslovakia from the I.M.F. in 1954, although the Fund at the time — with Czechoslovakia the last socialist country to be a Member and the bulk of the developing world not yet independent — may have represented the mutually congenial rather than all mankind. For a detailed description of these discussions, see Gold, p. 49, note 11 above, at 345-72.

outlook; major deviation may there be sufficiently disturbing to the work of the organization or the functioning of its institutions to warrant separation from the offender.[26]

2. *Representation*

There are circumstances — of which the existence of two rival authorities is the most obvious, but certainly not the only one — in which it is necessary for an international organization to determine who may, for its purposes, represent a Member. Such a determination should be related, precisely, to the purposes of the organization. Again, however, the issue is confused by attitudes, largely drawn from inter-State relations, which tend to restrict the independent authority of the organization.

One aspect of the confusion has been the controversy whether organizations may consider problems of representation as such or whether they are concerned only with the formal validity of credentials — the "full powers" of international relations. The legal issue reflected by the controversy is whether organizations, the constitutions of which contain no express provision on the subject, have the implied power to inquire into questions of representation. A practical adjunct of that issue — and a partial answer thereto — lies in the fact that problems of representation may arise in cases, activities or bodies in which there is no verification of credentials or in which formal verification alone provides no answer. A recent review of the matter with reference to the United Nations concludes that, while practice has been uneven and politicized, the power to inquire into representation has, in one manner or another, been recognized there.[27] Of some interest also, as an example of attitudes in a specialized agency, may be the discussion of both the legal and practical issues in the Governing Body of the

[26] Such a view was reflected by the difficulties of the Organization of American States with Cuba in the early 1960s, of the Council of Europe with Greece in the late 1960s, and more recently of the Council of Europe with Turkey. In the institutional structure of the Council of Europe, the existence of a parliamentary body chosen by national parliamentarians, however limited its authority, appears to require a certain type of democratic society of its Members.

[27] D. Ciobanu, "Credentials of Delegations and Representation of Member States at the U.N.", 25 *I.C.L.Q.* 351 (1976). See also J. Verhoeven, *La reconnaissance internationale dans la pratique contemporaine* (1975), p. 449.

International Labour Office in November 1971.[28] In October 1971 the General Assembly of the United Nations had decided to recognize the Government of the People's Republic as the only legitimate representative of China in the United Nations. The Secretary-General of the United Nations informed the specialized agencies of that decision and drew their attention to the fact that General Assembly Resolution 396(V) (to be considered below) had recommended that the attitude of the General Assembly in matters of representation should be taken into account in the specialized agencies. In the I.L.O. the matter was brought before the Governing Body — which has no credentials procedure — by the Director-General on the ground that, if there were not to be a sharp divergence between the position in the I.L.O. and in the United Nations pending the following session of the International Labour Conference eight months later, it was necessary to consider the action to be taken regarding the representation of China in the Governing Body itself and in an Asian Regional Conference, as well as for purposes of Office communications. During a lengthy discussion in the Governing Body it was tacitly accepted by all and expressly stated by some[29] that the I.L.O. had implied competence to determine which authority represented a Member State and that this competence was distinct from the verification of credentials. Controversy focused on the organ able to exercise the competence: in the view of some only the Conference, as the organ representative of all Member States, could deal with such an issue; according to others the Governing Body had the requisite powers to act, because of the urgency of the matter and because its own composition was, *inter alia*, at issue.[30] By 35 votes to 10, the Governing Body decided that it was able to deal with the matter.[31]

[28] Minutes of the 184th Session of the Governing Body, pp. 7-36, 116-21.

[29] Minutes of the 184th Session of the Governing Body, pp. 20, 22, 27-8.

[30] For the composition of the Regional Conference, the Governing Body could be taken to have express authority: under the rules relating to such conferences, the Governing Body determines "which governments" shall be invited to nominate delegates.

[31] In U.N.E.S.C.O. the matter was also dealt with by the Executive Board at its 88th Session (Oct.-Nov. 1971) (the next Conference session being a year later); there also there was question as to the Board's competence. In I.C.A.O. the decision was taken by the Council in November 1971, subject to the approval of the following session of the Assembly (three years later). In W.H.O., the Executive Board in January 1972 referred the matter to the World Health Assembly in May

Another element of confusion has been the relation between representation in the organization and the recognition of Governments by Member States.[32] Since changes in Government are more frequent than the emergence of new international entities, the matter is of much greater importance in connection with representation than in connection with membership. Some of the difficulties of basing international action on national recognition policies are obvious. To begin with, it is conceivable that representatives of a Member be appointed by an authority other than a Government. For instance, in 1960 the General Assembly, by Resolution 1498 (XV), accepted the credentials of the representatives of the Republic of the Congo (Leopoldville) "issued by the Head of State"; credentials similarly issued were accepted, despite objections, at the 1961 Session of the International Labour Conference. Further, there is the problem of rival authorities claiming to be the government of a Member: in an early case of the problem of representation of a Member in the International Labour Conference — that relating to Yugoslavia in 1944 — the Credentials Committee found that the Government which had appointed the delegation was generally recognized by Member States; however, it advised the Conference that it was "impressed with the difficulties which would have confronted it if there had been divergences between the recognition policies of the different Members of the Organization".[33] In the United Nations a 1950 memorandum of the Secretary-General on legal aspects of problems of representation,[34] which was a response to the first United Nations case of two rival authorities claiming to be entitled to represent a Member State, referred to an additional practical problem, namely that the "head-count" of Members which had recognized a particular authority might vary between organs and

with a recommendation for action; there apparently was no problem of representation in an organ or at meetings during the intervening period, but the Director-General was authorized to communicate with the Government of the People's Republic.

32 Keeping the notions of representation and recognition apart is not facilitated by a tendency to regard decisions on representation as recognition by the organization. See, for a striking example of this, *U.N.J.Y.B.* 1972, p. 155.

33 Record of Proceedings of the 26th Session of the International Labour Conference, pp. 292-2.

34 U.N. Document S/1466; Official Records of the Security Council, 5th Year, suppl. For Jan-May 1950, pp. 18-23.

might, as regards the Security Council, be determined by the arbitrary fact of election to serve at a given time. The more essential issue stated in that memorandum is that it would appear to be "legally inadmissible" to condition representation in an international body on recognition — often regarded as a political decision — by individual Members. General Assembly Resolution 396(V), which was the outcome of the consideration, in 1950, of the question of "Recognition by the United Nations of the representation of a Member State", and which declares that the attitude adopted by the General Assembly on such a question "shall not of itself affect the direct relations of individual Member States with the State concerned", nevertheless does not deal expressly with the relevance of the recognition policies of Members to the attitude of the General Assembly. It may be that the current spread of the policy of not taking any formal decision to recognize governments will make it easier in future for organizations to concentrate on their own concerns.

What should be those concerns, in relation to the participation of Members in the regular work of the organization (*i.e.* leaving out of account representation for particular purposes such as Security Council discussion of conflicts producing rival authorities)? In the above-mentioned 1950 memorandum of the Secretary-General the view was expressed that, by analogy to the requirements for the admission of States in Article 4 of the Charter, the test should be the ability to carry out the obligations of the Charter. Such a test of effectiveness was already envisaged in the League of Nations[35] and at various suitable times reference has been made to it since.[36] Yet

[35] See H. Lauterpacht, "The Credentials of the Abyssinian Delegation to the Seventeenth Assembly of the League of Nations", 18 *B.Y.* 184 (1937). The author indicates that the report of the Credentials Committee of the Assembly implied that the Assembly might refuse to recognize the credentials of the delegation if it were definitely established that there no longer was an independent government exercising authority on behalf of the Emperor, points out that it might be a matter of dispute how far the Assembly was entitled, by laying down the condition of effectiveness, to question the legality of credentials issued by the lawful sovereign of a Member, and suggests that the solution would be voluntary abstention from participation.

[36] See, e.g., 68 *A.J.I.L.* 318 (1974), the U.S. brief on Khmer representation: "the question ... is not one of recognition, which may involve a variety of political and other subjective factors, but rather one of the objective realities of effective authority and ability to fulfil the obligations of the Charter on behalf of the Member State". For an examination of U.N. practice in the light of the principle

General Assembly Resolution 396(V) — perhaps under the influence of the specific case then under consideration — makes no reference to effectiveness: it "recommends that, whenever more than one authority claims to be the government entitled to represent a Member State in the United Nations and this question becomes the subject of controversy in the United Nations, the question should be considered in the light of the Purposes and Principles of the Charter and the circumstances of each case". And it is difficult to affirm that United Nations practice has shown attachment to a principle of effectiveness seeing that for over twenty years the access to the organization of the authority effectively governing the largest population in the world was barred. One is tempted to wonder whether, in a world in which questions of representation in international organizations were wholly detached from political issues of recognition of governments, it might be conceivable that rival authorities governing different portions of the same State with some permanence could participate in organizations, each in respect of its portion, without this prejudging the unity of the State.[37]

The interplay, in respect of representation in international organizations, of political considerations, on the one hand, and the needs of the organization, on the other, poses another dilemma. One of the purposes of General Assembly Resolution 396(V) was to ensure that there were no conflicting decisions by various organs of the United Nations and that priority of decision was given to the General Assembly, as the organ "in which consideration can best be given to the views of all Member States in matters affecting the functioning of the Organization as a whole". At the same time, the General Assembly recommended that its attitude should be taken into account in the specialized agencies. The specialized agencies have followed that recommendation and have taken the view that representation is a political matter in respect of

of effectiveness, see E. Sciso, "La questione delle credenziali cambogiane all Assemblea generale delle Nazione Unite", *Riv. dir. int.* 1981, p. 83, and the note on Cambodian representation, 15 *Harvard Int'l L.J.* 495 (1974).

[37] Although it was formally a question of membership, the fact that, in most specialized agencies, one German Government and one Vietnamese Government claimed to represent the whole country without having effective authority over the whole territory made the situation of these countries somewhat akin to that of China.

which it is appropriate to leave the decision to the main political organization. Such an approach certainly reduces controversy in the agencies. However, it is possible to look at the question from the opposite point of view, namely that in organizations with technical concerns representation does not need to be a political issue and that, accordingly, the decision of such organizations might properly be different from that of the United Nations. It may be recalled that in 1950 the Executive Committee of the U.P.U. accepted for "technical reasons" that the Government of the People's Republic could represent China, although that decision was later reversed. Also, representation has differing implications in various organizations: for instance, it has been pointed out that for Members of I.C.A.O. the Chicago Convention on International Civil Aviation creates mutual rights and obligations for the application of which governments are responsible in their jurisdiction;[38] ability and willingness to give effect to these obligations thus take on a particular importance.

There remains, again, the question whether there may be "non-recognition" by an international organization for reasons of its own. It has been suggested above, in connection with membership, that it may be appropriate for organizations to refuse to take cognizance of legal situations which owe their existence to violation of a fundamental principle of the international community. Somewhat incoherently, the practice of organizations with regard to representation appears to bear out that view. At the same time, it appears to be widely felt that a distinction should be drawn, in this connection, between situations in which the organization can choose among rival authorities and cases where only one authority claims to represent a Member.

Where there are two rival authorities the matter is considered in the United Nations, in accordance with General Assembly Resolution 396(V), "in the light of the Purposes and Principles of the Charter". This clearly permits account to be taken of violations of those purposes and principles. The decisions, since 1979, to continue to seat the representatives of the former Government of Democratic Kampuchea and not those of the authorities in effective control of Cambodia, on the ground that the latter were installed by the military intervention of Vietnam, would seem to be an example

[38] R.H. Mankiewicz, "Organisation de l'aviation civile internationale", 18 *Ann. Français* 1972, p. 804 at 804-7.

of this. The decisions have been supported by countries, such as the United Kingdom, which do not recognize the authorities appointing the representatives as a legitimate government.[39] At the same time, it poses the question of the appropriateness of giving representation to authorities with no effective jurisdiction, such as governments in exile.[40] An Indian proposal, in 1979, that the Cambodian seat be left vacant was not adopted; the view of the United Kingdom was that an "empty seat solution" was unacceptable on grounds of principle and precedent.[41]

That is the problem also with respect to situations in which no choice of authorities is available. Overwhelmingly, it is the view of legal authors[42] and, apparently, of governments[43] that the right of representation cannot be denied to the sole, effective government of a Member State. That view has been justified in advice by the

[39] See, e.g., the following Government statement (in the House of Lords) reproduced in 52 *B.Y.* 397 (1981):

> We need to make it clear to Vietnam that her attempt to occupy Cambodia and impose an unrepresentative Government on that country is not acceptable to the international community. Accordingly, ... we have felt it necessary to maintain the existing position on the Cambodian seat at the U.N. Our own position is of course clear. We withdrew recognition from the Pol Pot regime in December 1979. (*Ibid.*)

[40] The question whether a government in exile can sit in the United Nations was already considered, inconclusively, at the 28th session of the General Assembly, in 1973, in relation to Cambodia. It was the issue in the League of Nations, in 1937, with respect of Ethiopia. During the second world war, governments in exile of countries occupied by Germany attended meetings of the International Labour Conference in 1941 and 1944; the only problem was that concerning Yugoslavia, mentioned above.

[41] See Geoffrey Marston, ed., "United Kingdom Materials on International Law 1980", 51 *B.Y.* 355, 388 (1980).

[42] See, e.g., Blix, p. 52, note 21 above. "The State which is a member of [international] organizations is entitled to be represented in them through its Government. If, due to non-recognition, the authority legally constituting the Government were prevented from representing the State, a denial of a right on its part could be said to take place." (*Ibid.*, p. 689). Elsewhere, he states that non-recognition is not possible as regards relations necessary under the constitutions of international organizations with authorities which fulfil the international law criteria of governments (*ibid.*, p. 693); this seems to imply that the existence of a rival to an effective government is not relevant. See also Ciobanu, and see Verhoeven, p. 54, note 27 above.

[43] This would appear to be the reason why the credentials of the Government of Afghanistan have not been formally challenged in recent years. An objection was submitted by Pakistan at the 1984 session of the International Labour Conference, but after the expiry of the statutory time limits.

Legal Counsel of the United Nations[44] on the ground that a refusal to seat the representatives of the sole government would have the effect of suspending a Member State from the exercise of rights and privileges of membership in a manner not provided for in the Charter. In the I.L.O., in 1958, the Chairman of the Credentials Committee similarly described such refusal as tantamount to temporary expulsion.[45] Yet that position is not wholly convincing or satisfying. There are, in fact, circumstances in which no representatives of a Member State are seated, for reasons unconnected with deliberate non-recognition: for instance, in 1965 the Credentials Committee of the International Labour Conference took the view, by reference to the fact that the United Nations Security Council had unanimously endorsed the conclusion of the Secretary-General that it was unclear which of two contending authorities in the Dominican Republic could be regarded as the government, that "it is not at present able to conclude that either the 'constitutional Government' or the 'Government of National Reconstruction' is competent validly to communicate the composition of a delegation" and that, consequently, "the Dominican Republic cannot at this stage be considered as being represented at this session of the Conference".[46] From the point of view of the principle of effectiveness — which is relied upon where there is only one authority and which has, after all, a great deal to do with the dividing line between reality and fiction — the seating of representatives of a government in exile leaves the State in question as unrepresented as one in which there is no alternative to the unacceptable effective government.[47] And there is something shocking, from the point of view of legal principle, in the different treatment of identical legal situations according to whether the need to ensure the presence of the Member State can be met by

[44] Document A/8160, Official Records of the 25th Session of the General Assembly, Annexes, Item 3, p. 3; *U.N.J.Y.B.* 1970, pp. 169-71. Ciobanu, see p. 54, note 27 above, relies on the provisions regarding expulsion and the respective authority of the Security Council and the General Assembly in relation thereto. It should be noted that Res. 396(V) does not apply to cases in which there is no rival authority.

[45] Record of Proceedings of the 42nd Session of the International Labour Conference, pp. 493-4.

[46] Record of Proceedings of the 49th Session of the International Labour Conference, pp. 494-5.

[47] This point is made by Verhoeven, see p. 54, note 27 above.

finding some participants, however unsatisfactory they may be. It is likely that, in the present state of the constitutional law of organizations, denial of any representation to a Member State is improper. It is certain that, in such cases as there have been of denial of representation — with respect to Hungary in the International Labour Conference in 1958-59 and with respect to South Africa in the United Nations since 1974 — the legal issues involved, including that of the nature of legal violations which could lead to "non-recognition", have not been properly explored. Nevertheless, it is permissible to wonder whether a distinction between, on the one hand, continued membership to which the considerations regarding expulsion set out above apply, and, on the other hand, temporary non-representation may not, in particular and hopefully exceptional circumstances, be warranted from the point of view of the credibility of the legal order of international organizations.[48]

3. Participation and Representativity

The quality and efficacy of the work of international organizations is likely to be influenced by the manner in which and the extent to which participation therein reflects the interest of the entities represented in the activities of the organization.[49] This has two aspects which may overlap. One is the reflection of sectoral interests in activities of particular concern to the sectors in question. The other is the degree of interest in matters of more universal concern. Neither, except in an organization such as the United Nations concerned with questions of war and peace, has anything directly to do with power.

The question of the appropriate representation of sectoral interests may arise at different levels. There are organizations which exist only for the defence of a particular interest and in which this is reflected in membership. For instance, the Organization of

[48] That this may not be possible under present constitutions would then merely be one further example of the lack of "teeth" given to organizations for the defence of their principles. See more generally in "inactive membership" K. Ginther, *Berichte der Deutschen Gesellschaft für Völkerrecht*, vol. 17 (1975).

[49] Literature on the subject is largely concerned with voting arrangements. See, for instance, S. Zamora, "Voting in International Economic Organizations", 74 *A.J.I.L.* 566 (1980); W. Gold, "Weighted Voting Power: Some Limits and Some Problems", 68 *A.J.I.L.* 687 (1974).

Petroleum Exporting Countries expressly prohibits the admission, even to associate membership, of a country "which does not fundamentally have interests and aims similar to those of Member countries". There are organizations which exist essentially for the purpose of balancing two interests. Key examples of such organizations are the Councils established under Commodity Agreements: in them the membership is divided into exporters and importers, with equal voting power, and relative importance within each of these two groups is then taken into account in the distribution of votes within the group.[50] Some organizations essentially concerned with business-type activities take account, both in voting arrangements and in the composition of limited organs, of the shares held by different countries in operating capital; the main examples of this are international and regional banks. The difficulty of taking adequate account of particular interests increases with the range of the activities of an organization and the size of its membership. Some organizations with competence in technical fields reflect a degree of concern with certain aspects of these fields in the composition of their executive organs; this is the case, for instance, of I.C.A.O. and I.M.O. There may be subsidiary bodies with activities limited to particular sectors, the composition of which takes account of interest in these sectors; this is the case, for instance, with the I.L.O. Industrial Committees. But there would appear to be no magic formula of representation or voting which can ensure that, in universal organizations with multiple activities, appropriate account will in every case be automatically taken of particular interests involved.[51]

It is also extremely difficult, in organizations with wide-ranging activities, to define with precision the nature of particular interests which merit special standing, in the composition of organs, in voting or otherwise. The best known case of a problem in this

[50] A similar arrangement balances the interests of two groups of providers and one group of receivers in I.F.A.D. See also the provisions for representation in the Council of the proposed Seabed Authority.

[51] A percentage of failures resulting from the fact that particular concerns are not sufficiently taken into account — such as standards on permanent representatives not acceptable to host countries or on migrant workers not acceptable to immigration countries — is then, if not inevitable, no more than a reflection of human inadequacy, whether in negotiation or in preparation — the "margin of error" known in business activities.

respect, that of the *Constitution of the Maritime Safety Committee of the Inter-Governmental Maritime Consultative Organization* which came before the International Court of Justice in 1960,[52] is generally recalled for its importance in the law of "vires". At the same time, it raised two substantive issues regarding the requirement that the Committee "consist of 14 Members elected by the Assembly from Members, governments having an important interest in maritime safety, of which not less than eight shall be the largest ship-owning nations . . ." First, if, as the Court found, the text implied an important interest in maritime safety of the largest ship-owning nations, what was the intended nature of that interest? The traditional maritime countries assumed that a text drafted in the mid 1940s — *i.e.* before the emergence of "flags of convenience" as a major factor in world shipping — was directed to the knowledgeable concern of countries actively administering major fleets: from that point of view membership in the Committee of Liberia and Panama could at the time be considered as not satisfying the intent of the provision. However, it could equally be argued that it was essential to involve in international co-operation regarding maritime safety any country which had the opportunity to play a major role in that field, even if it was not yet taking active advantage of that opportunity.[53] Second, how was "ship-owning" by a nation to be measured? As long as private ownership and registration largely coincided, statistics of registered tonnage provided a universally acceptable basis for measurement. As soon as they diverged, the question whether registration or actual or beneficial ownership was more important became relevant. The Court did address itself to this question. It held that there must be objective criteria — although the United Kingdom and the Netherlands had argued that the fact that "ship-owning" had no clear-cut meaning implied that discretionary evaluation was possible — and that registered tonnage was indicated as appropriate by a variety of *indicia*; beneficial interest (which had been proposed

[52] *I.C.J. Reports* 1960, p. 150; 30 *I.L.R.* 426.

[53] An analogous argument took place in the I.L.O. regarding the (discretionary) composition of technical conferences preparatory to maritime sessions of the General Conference. Traditionally, they were limited to the thirty or so countries having the largest registered tonnage. However, it was pointed out that developing countries building up merchant fleets could benefit particularly from the discussions at the preparatory meetings.

by Norway) was difficult to ascertain, uncertain and without basis in international practice.

Another picture of the difficulty of accurately defining particular interests, even where express provision is made for them, is provided by the periodic consideration and evolution over time of the concept of "States of chief industrial importance" which have non-elective seats in the I.L.O. Governing Body. It is clear from the preparatory work of the original Constitution of the I.L.O. (Part XIII of the Treaty of Versailles) that "industrial" was used in the widest sense, covering all occupations and particularly including agriculture. Nevertheless, the first choice of States of chief industrial importance, in 1919, was made on narrower criteria: persons employed in industry; horsepower, in total and per head of population; length of railways; and merchant marine. The result was challenged by a number of countries and particularly India. After two years' examination of possible alternatives, India was included amongst the Members of chief industrial importance for reasons which were not clearly specified. In 1934 new criteria were adopted: contributions to the Organization; industrial importance in the narrow sense as measured by the 1919 criteria; foreign trade; and total gainfully occupied population; the first three were given weights of 3 and the last of 1. Another major change came in 1948, the criteria and weights then adopted being contributions to the Organization (8); national income (4); foreign trade (4); and gainfully occupied population (1). At the same time, a Committee of statistical experts cast doubt on some of these criteria: in their final report, the experts expressed the view that "the test of industrial importance is the contribution that the economy of a given country makes both to its own people and to the world, in terms of physical goods, industrial and agricultural, and of services such as welfare, transport, distribution, etc."; they considered that neither the contribution to the Organization nor foreign trade was a valid measure of industrial importance as so defined. In 1954 all the criteria were retained — contributions and trade as being useful as long as statistics of national income were not fully reliable — but the weights of the first three were reduced to 3, 3 and 1. In 1963 the criterion of foreign trade was dropped; the weight of (net) national income was raised to 6. Contributions to the Organization were dropped as a criterion in 1978 and the relationship of (net) national income to active population fixed at 4 or 3[54] to 1. Finally, in 1983, gross national product[55] was taken alone, as reflecting also the size of the labour force. What underlies the various permutations of criteria and weights is the tension between, on the one hand, national wealth and, on the other, size of population and labour force. With the independence of populous segments of old empires, and the rise on the world scene of major "semi-developed" countries such as Brazil, the tension acquired a political significance it did not have in earlier years. To some extent, as in the problem of the ship-owning States in I.M.C.O., it is a conflict between the legitimate claims of the existing and the potential.

So analysed the difficulties encountered in the application of specific provisions regarding sectoral interests in organizations with wide-ranging activities are but a foretaste of the problems liable to be encountered in any attempt at measuring, behind the facade of the sovereign equality of States, the degree of real interest in matters of universal concern. Yet, in the face of phenomena such as the emergence of micro-States and conflicts, in international organizations, between the developed "North" and the more numerous developing "South", various governments and theorists are searching for some measure which would justify, perhaps, differential membership rights,[56] or weighted voting or simply the publication[57] of the real weight of international decisions.

There are various temptations to be resisted. In particular, while large contributors are entitled to some assurance that they will not be subjected to excessive burdens by those who pay less and that the

[54] Both weights then produced the same result.

[55] Gross national product is used as a basis for weighting votes in Eurocontrol.

[56] See, e.g., M.M. Gunter, "What Happened to the U.N. Ministate Problem?" 71 *A.J.I.L.* 110 (1977) for an analysis of U.S. and United Kingdom proposals and legal advice relating thereto.

[57] L.B. Sohn ["Due Process in the U.N. 69 *A.J.I.L.*" 62 (1975)] has suggested that without introducing any system of weighted voting, the United Nations computer which tabulates the votes might be programmed to include data relating to each State's population and gross national product. The General Assembly could then authorize the Secretary-General to announce, when so requested by at least ten States, not only the number of States which voted for or against a resolution but also the percentages of the world population and world gross product which are represented by the States voting for or against the resolution. In this manner the claims of alleged non-representativeness of the majority behind a particular resolution could be easily resolved (*ibid.*, at p. 622).

money of their taxpayers will be well spent, one should be careful not to carry too far the notion that "he who pays the piper calls the tune". On the international as on the national plane, considerations of cost are only one element to be taken into account in determining the activities to be carried out; ability to pay is a limited criterion, even of wealth; and the acknowledged need for balanced development everywhere, as well as the right of different countries — as long as there are nation States — to decide, in the last resort, how to approach their own development, makes this an area in which too great an encroachment on sovereign equality raises a variety of issues of principle.

Population is a neutral criterion. On the national plane, it tends to be the basis for the delimitation of electoral constituencies and hence the basis of representative government. In the two Western European international organizations which have parliamentary bodies[58] — the Council of Europe and the European Communities — population plays an analogous role in the composition of the bodies, but these as yet have limited authority. More widely, population cannot be used as the sole or even main basis for representation for a variety of reasons, including the fact that population is most unevenly distributed by States and even continents. In view of this, the formula agreed[59] after many years of negotiation for the composition of the Government group of the I.L.O. Governing Body, to replace the present arrangement reserving seats for States of chief industrial importance,[60] is of some interest.[61] Under that formula the number of seats reserved for each one of four geographical regions [Africa, America, Asia (including the Pacific) and Europe] would be determined, within a limited range, by "the application of equal weighting of the number of States Members within the region, their total population and their economic activity assessed by appropriate criteria (gross national product or contributions to the budget of the

58 Other than the special case of the Nordic Council.

59 Although not yet formally adopted.

60 The present arrangement meets opposition both on grounds of principle — ten seats being non-elective — and for practical reasons — one continent, Africa, having no continuity of representation under it.

61 For details of the formula, see, for instance, Record of Proceedings of the 69th Session of the International Labour Conference (1983), pp. 2/9-11.

Organization)".[62] Each region (which may, as in the case of Europe, be further split into sub-regions dividing the allotted seats between them) would have its own electoral college, and each such college

> shall take the necessary steps to ensure that a substantial number of Members appointed to fill the seats assigned to that region is chosen on the basis of the importance of their population and that an equitable geographical distribution is assured while at the same time taking into consideration other factors such as the economic activity of the Members concerned in accordance with the special characteristics of the region.

The manner of so doing is to be decided by regional protocols. The proposed Protocol agreed by the States of Western Europe would determine the "share of each State" in the seats allocated to it by "the fraction it represents of the total of the States of Western Europe based on application of the following three criteria which will be equally weighted: the number of States, their population and their contributions".[63] States may form groups to pool their shares and agree among themselves on the filling of seats to which this would entitle them; where one State has a share greater than one seat, the excess would be redistributed proportionately amongst other States or groups. A test assessment of the formula on the basis of 1982 statistics would give a share of a full seat to France and the Federal Republic of Germany, as well as to a grouping of Scandinavian States corresponding to the one existing at present.[64]

B. Non-Governmental Participants

A former legal counsel of the United Nations has stated: "It is obvious that, if international organizations are to be effective, they must make provision for the participation of all those actors whose support is necessary for political success. Many non-State actors are

[62] The initial distribution would be: America, 12 seats; Africa, 13 seats; Europe and Asia, alternatively 14 and 15 seats.

[63] Under present arrangements, the relative weighting of (economically active) population to criteria of wealth has never been higher than 1 to 3.

[64] The United Kingdom's share of a seat — 0.97% — would probably be brought to a full seat by distribution of excess. On the other hand, Italy, at present a "State of chief industrial importance", would have a share of only 0.88% and Spain at present among the leading claimants to be a State of chief industrial importance, of 0.58%.

now effective; hence their participation must be provided for ..."[65] At the same time, the more active participation becomes, the more relevant are the terms of representation and the question how the representativity of "non-State actors" is to be determined.

1. Liberation Movements[66]

The participation of liberation movements in the work of certain international organizations — largely of the U.N. family — had its beginnings in a problem of representation. Following recommendations of the U.N. Economic Commission for Africa, in its resolutions 42(IV) and 68(V), the Economic and Social Council decided on 30 July 1963, by Resolution 974(XXXVI), to exclude Portugal from membership of the Commission; it further decided to give associate membership in the Commission to dependent territories in Africa. This meant that a solution had to be found for the representation of the territories under Portuguese administration as associate Members.[67] Initial legal advice by the United Nations Secretariat was that representation was a matter for the administering authority[68] and for some time the matter rested there. However, at its eighth Session, the Economic Commission for Africa proposed that the Organization for African Unity be asked to designate representatives of the "populations" concerned, and at its ninth Session suggested a procedure under which O.A.U. proposals would be submitted to the General Assembly. In 1971, by Resolution 2795(XXVI), the General Assembly approved these arrangements regarding the representation of territories under Portuguese administration as well as the list of the representatives proposed by the O.A.U.

Once their capacity to represent the Portuguese-administered territories in the Economic Commission for Africa had been

[65] E. Suy, "Status of Observers in International Organizations", 160 *R.C.A.D.I.* 1978-II, p. 75.

[66] For relevant literature, see in particular C. Lazarus, "Le Statut des Mouvements de Liberation Nationale à L'Organisation des Nations Unies", 20 *Ann. Français* 1974, p. 173; J.A. Barberis, "Nouvelles Questions concernant la personnalité juridique internationale", 56 *R.C.A.D.I.* 1983-I, p. 145.

[67] As expressly noted in Resolution 974(XXXVI), the States responsible for the international relations of other territories accepted associate membership.

[68] Doc. E/3963.

accepted in this manner, the liberation movements in question were the first in respect of whom the issue of participation arose elsewhere. Thus a resolution adopted by the International Labour Conference in June 1972 invited the Governing Body to examine "the most appropriate ways of enabling representatives of Angola, Mozambique and Guinea (Bissau), which are associate Members of the Economic Commission for Africa, to participate in I.L.O. meetings, and in particular in I.L.O. African Regional Conferences". An Office paper to the 188th Session of the Governing Body[69] suggested that the normal procedure was to invite an observer delegation from a non-self-governing territory through the administering power; it was not within the competence of the I.L.O. to determine the representative character of liberation movements and, as the Secretary-General had pointed out in his report to the 26th Session of the General Assembly,

> it would be for the General Assembly to examine, in the first instance, to what extent it may be necessary and desirable to create a new category of participant. This would involve, *inter alia*, the question of the status of liberation movements in regard to representation, under international law, of the territories concerned.

By the time the matter was considered in the Governing Body, the General Assembly had affirmed, in Resolution 2918(XXVII), that the national liberation movements of the territories under Portuguese administration were the authentic representatives of the "true aspirations" of the peoples in question and had recommended that, *inter alia*, the specialized agencies should ensure the representation of these territories by the movements concerned in an appropriate capacity. Despite legal reservations by some, this was considered sufficient guidance by the Governing Body; at its 190th Session,[70] in June 1973, it decided to invite the movements in question to the International Labour Conference and to African regional conferences as observers.

In the U.N. General Assembly the ground was prepared for the attendance of the movements in question as observers by the decision,

[69] Minutes of the 188th Session of the Governing Body (November 1972), pp. 132-3.

[70] Minutes of the 190th Session of the Governing Body (May-June 1973), pp. 52-7, 238.

in 1973, to approve the credentials of the delegation of Portugal "on the clear understanding that they represent Portugal as it exists within its frontiers in Europe . . ."[71] In the same year, by Resolution 3151 (XXVIII) G, the General Assembly created a representation problem regarding South Africa by declaring that its regime had no right to represent its people. As regards Namibia and Zimbabwe, the non-recognition of the right of the authorities in power to represent the territories in question was understood.[72] The way was thus clear for Resolution 3280(XXIX) inviting the liberation movement of the various areas in question to participate as observers, *inter alia*, in all main Committees of the Assembly.[73] The invitation, also in 1974, to the Palestine Liberation Organization[74] was based on a more complex problem of representation — a problem of represention nonetheless.[75]

Since the invitations to liberation movements thus constituted a question of representation, the admission of Namibia, represented by the U.N. Council for Namibia, to a number of organizations, posed the problem of the role of the Namibian liberation movement S.W.A.P.O.[76] In the I.L.O., for instance, the view was taken that it was thereafter a matter for the Council to decide on the integration of S.W.A.P.O. into the delegation of Namibia; in practice this has been done by treating S.W.A.P.O. as representative of Namibia's workers and appointing a member of the movement as Workers' delegate. Other organizations have not been so rigidly logical, and have permitted S.W.A.P.O. to send observers, in addition to the delegates appointed by the Council.

All the decisions of the United Nations regarding liberation movements were based on the recognition of these movements by

[71] G.A. Res. 3181(XXVIII), 1973. In the I.L.O., the Credentials Committee of the 58th Session of the Conference, in 1973 — after the liberation movements of Portuguese-administered territories had been admitted — held that the Portuguese Workers' delegate did not represent the workers of those territories.

[72] See also the specific recognition of S.W.A.P.O., in 1973, in U.N. Res. 3111 (XXVIII), and the same year of Z.A.P.U. and Z.A.N.U., in Res. 3115(XXVIII).

[73] In practice, they had been invited earlier, in particular to the Fourth Committee.

[74] U.N. Res. 3237(XXIX).

[75] See in particular U.N. Res. 2787(XXVI) and 3236(XXIX).

[76] The problem existed earlier in that the U.N. Council's responsibilities formally included that of appointing representatives of Namibia to international meetings; it became more acute with full membership.

regional organizations. Thus General Assembly Resolution 3280 (XXIX) deals with co-operation between the United Nations and the Organization of African Unity, and the paragraph on the invitation of liberation movements refers to the movements "recognized by the Organization of African Unity". It is often asserted that the decision to recognize the Palestine Liberation Organization was taken by the General Assembly itself; however, Resolution 3237(XXIX), which gave that organization observer status, refers back to Resolution 3102(XXVIII) which urged that the "national liberation movements recognized by the various regional intergovernmental organizations concerned" be invited to the Diplomatic Conference on humanitarian law. In the International Labour Organization the original *ad hoc* decision concerning the liberation movements of Portuguese-administered territories in Africa was expressly based on their recognition by the United Nations. However, when it became apparent that the role of liberation movements would not be as temporary as thought at first, provisions were inserted in the Standing Orders of the General Conference and of regional conferences which refer to liberation movements recognized by the Organization of African Unity or the League of Arab States.[77] Similarly, in U.N.E.S.C.O., the amendments to the rules of procedure adopted at the 18th Session of the General Conference (1974) refer, on the one hand, to "African liberation movements recognised by the Organization of African Unity" and, on the other, to "the Palestine Liberation Organization, recognized by the League of Arab States".

What is the nature of the process of "recognition" so delegated, in effect, to certain regional organizations? It has clearly been for those organizations to say which movements might be considered to be representative of the populations of certain territories. The Organization of African Unity established procedures for that purpose which were described as follows by H.M. Blix in 1970:

> Such movements are recognized . . . provided that they are really effective within an area. This is ascertained partly by inquiries with the neighbours, partly by the sending of fact-finding officers to the areas in question. Full

[77] There was some divergence of views on this reference. See Record of Proceedings of the 66th Session of the International Labour Conference (1975), pp. 38, 205 and 239. Some subsidiary organs of the U.N. continue to rely on decisions by the General Assembly alone.

> control of a portion of territory is not required ... There is no obstacle to the recognition of two movements within the same area, if they are both effective.[78]

The description is tantamount to a form of recognition of insurgency,[79] for a new purpose; like such recognition, the judgment may be somewhat subjective. The co-operation of the regional organizations (and particularly the O.A.U.) has also been of practical use in identifying the persons who sign the communications[80] appointing the representatives sent by liberation movements; while some movements have been so highly structured as to have "foreign ministers" others have been more loosely organized.

It is much less certain that it has been for those organizations also to determine in respect of which territories or populations liberation movements should be given recognition. The terms of General Assembly Resolution 3280(XXIX), as well as of the Standing Orders provisions adopted in the I.L.O. and in U.N.E.S.C.O. (as regards African movements), are wide enough to embrace this aspect also. However, as suggested above, all the liberation movements which have in practice participated in the work of international organizations have had a claim to be representative of populations in respect of which the General Assembly had, for one reason or another, decided that there was an issue of representation. The Organization of African Unity recognized certain liberation movements — for instance of the Comores and the Seychelles — which appear never to have played any representational role in the organizations of the United Nations family. The difference between them and the other movements would seem to have been that the territories to which they belonged were moving towards self-determination and that they were playing a role in constitutional processes to that end. Participation by liberation movements in international organizations, at least of the U.N. family, would thus seem to have been dependent on a double condition: a finding, by the United Nations, that a particular

[78] See Blix, p. 52. note 21 above, at p. 617.

[79] In a few cases liberation movements were recognized although they already had a constitutional place in the territory concerned, possibly for the purpose of channelling international aid to them.

[80] Such communications are not treated as credentials within the meaning of rules of procedure.

population was entitled, as an aspect of self-determination, to some form of distinct representation by persons able to speak for its aspirations; and the absence at the time, in the territory concerned, of constitutional procedures for the attainment of that end.

Such a conclusion nevertheless provides no guidance on the circumstances in which the double condition will be held to be met. The U.N. Declaration on the Granting of Independence to Colonial Countries and Peoples is clearly relevant; however, its application may not constitute the full or exclusive answer.[81] An interesting case is that of the Western Sahara (to which, according to the International Court of Justice, the Declaration is not inapplicable). General Assembly Resolution 34/37 of November 1979 refers to the Frente Polisario as representative of the people of the Western Sahara. Persons appointed by the movement are regularly heard by the Fourth Committee of the Assembly. However, it has apparently at no time been designated as a liberation movement by the Organization of African Unity[82] — despite a recommendation in 1976 of the O.A.U. liberation committee — or by the United Nations.

A further question which arises is whether it is possible for an organization to refuse to admit a liberation movement found by a regional organization to be representative of a population considered by the United Nations to be entitled to and unable to achieve self-determination. In the various *ad hoc* decisions as well as Standing Orders provisions regarding the participation of liberation movements, care has been taken to make such participation dependent on an invitation by the Organization; there is accordingly a margin of discretion. At the same time, attempts to establish some criteria for the exercise of the discretion have not been successful. Thus, in 1975, in connection with the adoption of Standing Orders provisions in the I.L.O., texts were proposed which would have variously required that liberation movements, in order to be invited, recognize the purposes and principles of the Charter of the United Nations, the principles of the I.L.O. and its Constitution and/or the right of all Member States to continue in

[81] See N. Ronzitti, "Wars of National Liberation — a Legal Definition", 1 *Italian Yearbook* 1975, pp. 192-205.

[82] In recent years the issue in the Organization has been whether the Western Sahara is an entity susceptible to be admitted to membership.

existence and participate in the work of the Organization.[83] These texts were not accepted in part because they appeared to be aimed at one particular movement. Nevertheless, it may be legitimate to take the view that if liberation movements are, as suggested by some, invited as representatives of a "proto State" they should, like Members and Associate Members, demonstrate some commitment to the principles of the Organization.[84]

2. *Public International Organizations*[85]

Most major international organizations make provision, in their Constitutions or rules of procedure, for the participation of other public international organizations in at least some of their meetings. Relationship agreements between organizations usually make provision for such participation. Insofar as there is no express agreement, invitations to particular organizations are discretionary; common interests, in general or in regard to the subject matter of a meeting, are clearly relevant. One organization, F.A.O., early laid down guidelines for relationship agreements with organizations other than those of the United Nations family.[86] They set out both criteria to determine the nature of the other organization — it should have been set up by a convention between States; its governing body should be composed of Members designated by governments; its income should be made up mainly of contributions from governments; and it should have legal capacity to enter into agreements with other organizations — and factors to be taken into account when deciding whether to conclude an agreement. In particular, the aims and purposes of the organization should be in conformity with the general principles embodied in the Charter of the United Nations and the Constitution of F.A.O., and normally

[83] See, in particular, Record of Proceedings of the 60th Session of the International Labour Conference, pp. 238-9.

[84] Res. 2089(LXIII) of the U.N. Economic and Social Council, admitting the Palestine Liberation Organization to full membership in the Economic Commission for Western Asia, affirms that this would contribute to the purposes and aims of the Commission, without referring to any express commitment to these purposes and aims.

[85] See R.J. Dupuy, "Le droit des relations entre les organisations internationales", 100 *R.C.A.D.I.* 1960-II, p. 457.

[86] Report of the tenth session of the Conference, Appendix G.

the Members of the organization should be Members of at least one of the organizations of the United Nations family.

The meetings in respect of which provision for participation is generally made are those of the major organs or bodies of the various organizations. Access to smaller meetings is more restricted, if only so as to ensure that their members are not outnumbered. However, the attendance of particular international organizations at such meetings may be of value too. For that purpose it is necessary to define more strictly than otherwise the nature of common interests. This may be done in a relationship agreement: for instance, the agreement between I.L.O. and I.M.C.O. provides for representation, respectively, at the Maritime Safety Committee and the Joint Maritime Committee. Alternatively, the interest may be determined on an *ad hoc* basis: for instance, organizations involved in the preparation or implementation of codes of conduct for multinationals have been invited to I.L.O. meetings concerned with its Tripartite Declaration regarding Multinationals, Of particular interest are the arrangements made, under the express terms of particular conventions or by decisions of the competent organs, to associate in the work of bodies supervising the application of standards in the United Nations,[87] I.L.O.,[88] and the Council of Europe[89] organizations which have collaborated in the preparation of the standards or have adopted overlapping or related texts.

The status of international organizations when participating in the work of others is distinct from that of the different categories of observers. It is, however, variable and ill-defined. In general a right to participate in decisions is neither sought nor granted.[90] There

[87] Working group of E.C.O.S.O.C. on the Covenant on Economic, Social and Cultural Rights; Human Rights Committee; supervisory committees for the Conventions on the Elimination of all Forms of Racial Discrimination and Discrimination against Women.

[88] Committee of Experts on the Application of Conventions and Recommendations, with respect to instruments on indigenous and tribal populations, safety of seafarers, vocational training, rural workers' organizations, nursing personnel and migrant workers.

[89] Committee of independent experts on European Social Charter.

[90] Even the European Communities do not normally enjoy voting rights. There may however be organs of particular minor bodies on which other organizations have full membership; an example is the Programme Committee of the I.L.O. Centre for Advanced Technical and Vocational Training; another is the Councils of the U.N. University and of the University for Peace (see attachments to General Assembly Resolution 35/55).

may be a right to submit proposals, but these may need to be supported by government delegates in order to be put to the vote or even discussed. In some bodies, representatives of other organizations may participate freely in discussions while in others they may speak only when requested. To some extent these variations reflect the nature of the body, or meeting, but the contribution which may be made by the organizations represented is not always the primary concern in the decisions on relevant rules.

Once an organization is invited by another, the question arises by whom it should be represented. Looking at the issue from the point of view of the negotiation and conclusion of treaties, the International Law Commission stated in 1981 that "the matter of representation of international organizations raises new questions . . ."[91] and decided, in effect, to leave these to be answered by the rules of each organization. Representation of an organization at meetings of another is not usually comparable to the commitment of the organization by the conclusion of a treaty. There is, however, a similar absence of settled law. With few exceptions[92] there are no express rules on the subject. In the great majority of cases representation is by members of the Secretariat. On some occasions they have an express brief from other bodies.[93]

At the same time, there would seem to be room for some differentiation, according to the purpose of representation. For instance, in certain cases the I.L.O. is represented by a tripartite delegation appointed by the Governing Body. An examination of practice suggests that this is done, on the one hand, when subjects of special importance to the I.L.O. are considered in other fora[94] and, on the

[91] *Y.B.I.L.C.* 1981-II, Part Two p. 129.

[92] For instance, Regulations 51-3 of the General Regulations of W.M.O. deal with "representation at the sessions of other organizations".

[93] For instance, when the International Labour Conference was considering the instrument which became the Discrimination (Employment and Occupation) Convention, 1958, the representative of the United Nations transmitted comments by the Commission on Human Rights and the Commission on the Status of Women.

[94] Tripartite delegations attended the General Assembly in the early, formative years of the United Nations and in 1966 for a discussion of the industrialization of developing countries; within the framework of the U.N. Economic and Social Council, tripartite delegations attended the Council in 1948 for a discussion of freedom of association and collaborated with the Human Rights Commission in 1951 on the covenants on human rights; such delegations also attended the 1960 Conference on Safety of Life at Sea, the F.A.O. World Conference on

other hand, when an international instrument is elaborated jointly with another organization and an organ of that organization or a conference convened by it is finally called upon to adopt that instrument.[95] One purpose of such a delegation is to give employers and workers a voice in the proceedings of otherwise exclusively governmental bodies. But — and this is a more general consideration — it also tends to ensure that the organization represented is accorded fuller rights of participation in the deliberations than might otherwise be the case, with respect to matters in which it has a direct interest. A prerequisite for the effectiveness of such participation is a sufficient degree of prior agreement within the appointing organ to enable the delegation to act on its behalf.

Another example is that of the representation of bodies concerned with particular matters within one organization at the discussion of related questions in another. Thus members of the Apartheid Committee have recently been included in the U.N. delegation to the International Labour Conference when questions concerning apartheid in labour matters have been under discussion. It can only serve the interest of co-ordination for members of specialized bodies so to provide and obtain first-hand knowledge of points of view expressed in other fora. At the same time, questions may need to be resolved both regarding the authority to appoint and regarding the right to speak on behalf of the delegation representing the organization as a whole.

However that may be, there is no doubt that the sending organization alone determines the composition of its delegation. The receiving organization lays down the rules governing the scope of the activities of the delegation, subject to the requirements of inter-organization agreements. But there are no procedures for it to determine the representativity or authority of the delegation. This would seem to be of minor importance for as long as the internal structure of most organizations is monolithic and their representatives in other organizations have no power of decision. However, novel issues may be raised by the participation of organizations such

Agrarian and Rural Development in 1979 and the U.N. Conference on Science and Technology for Development in 1979.

95 Intergovernmental Conference on the Status of Teachers, 1966 (U.N.E.S.C.O.); International Conference on Training and Certification of Seafarers, 1978 (I.M.C.O.).

as the European Communities, with two centres of authority which may pursue divergent policies, in the work of other organizations on a footing equivalent to that of States.

3. Employers[96] *and Workers*

When, in 1919, provision was made in the Constitution of the International Labour Organization (Part XIII of the Treaty of Versailles) for the participation, in particular in the International Labour Conference, with decision-making power, of representatives of the employers and workers as well as of the governments of Member States, the importance of the method of choosing the non-governmental representatives was immediately realized. It was accordingly specified that the Members of the Organization undertook "to nominate nongovernmental delegates and advisers chosen in agreement with the industrial organizations, if such organizations exist, which are most representative of employers or workpeople, as the case may be, in their respective countries"; the text has remained unchanged.[97] Furthermore, provision was made for a procedure of scrutinizing credentials under which the Conference might, by two-thirds of the votes cast by the delegates present, refuse to admit any delegate or adviser "whom it deems not to have been nominated in accordance with this Article"; this procedure also remains unchanged.

There have been relatively few cases in which the credentials of employers' or workers' delegates have been invalidated.[98] In some cases there was no invalidiation, despite a proposal in that sense from some member(s) of the Credentials Committee,[99] because the

[96] The I.L.O. terminology is intended here to cover representatives of business, not necessarily in their capacity as employers.

[97] It was then paragraph 3 of Article 389 of the Treaty: it is now paragraph 5 of Article 3 of the Constitution. The text applies in terms only to the General Conference; it is applied in practice to other meetings to which governments appoint non-governmental delegates.

[98] The main cases concern the Workers' delegate of the Argentine in 1945; the Workers' delegate of Venezuela in 1950; the Hungarian Employers' and Workers' delegates from 1957 to 1959; and the South African Workers' delegate in 1963 (South Africa's participation in the Organization ceased the following year).

[99] Any proposal for invalidation from one "side" of the Credentials Committee is put to the vote in plenary, even if the majority of the Committee does not support such proposal.

necessary two-thirds majority in the Conference was not attained. There have also been some instances of the credentials procedure achieving its aim in a different manner, that of a change of delegate in the course of the session. Often the Credentials Committee has sought to give guidance on the means of attaining the purposes of the Constitution, rather than to "punish". However that may be, the interpretation and application of the relevant constitutional provisions over more than sixty years shed much light on the determination of representativity in relation to national employers and workers.

The question of the manner in which the constitutional provision had to be applied to a split trade union movement came before the Permanent Court of International Justice as early as 1922. The case concerned the Workers' delegate of the Netherlands who had been appointed on the joint proposal of three trade union confederations having, together, some 280,000 members; the appointment was contested by a fourth confederation which was, individually, the largest and accordingly maintained that it was solely entitled to nominate the delegate. In Advisory Opinion No. 1 the Court held that the appointment was in conformity with the requirements of the constitutional provision, by reference, *inter alia*, to the following considerations:

> The most representative organizations for this purpose are, of course, those organizations which best represent the employers and the workers respectively. What these organization are is a question to be decided in the particular case, having regard to the circumstances in each particular country at the time when the choice falls to be made. Numbers are not the only test of the representative character of the organization, but they are an important factor: other things being equal, the most numerous will be the most representative ... If ... in a particular country there exist several independent organizations representing the working classes, the Government must take all of them into consideration ... The aim of each government must ... be an agreement with all the most representative organizations of employers and workers as the case may be; that, however is only an ideal ... What is required of the governments is that they should do their best to effect an agreement which in the circumstances, may be regarded as the best for the purpose of ensuring the representation of the workers of the country.[100]

[100] *Designation of the Workers' Delegation for the Netherlands, P. C. I. J.*, Series B. No. 1 (1922): 1 *Ann. Dig.* 316.

These considerations have, over time, led countries like Belgium, France and the Netherlands, in which the trade union movement is divided, to establish, in agreement with all concerned, arrangements under which the post of delegate is held by a nominee of each of the different confederations in turn, while nominees of the others are included in the delegation as advisers.[101]

Another issue which arose early and remains of current interest is whether the non-governmental delegates to a meeting concerned with a particular sector of the economy, such as a maritime session of the General Conference, should be appointed in agreement with the central organization most representative of all workers, or with the organization most representative of the workers in the sector in question, particularly where the latter is not affiliated to the central organization. It is clearly desirable that those attending the meeting should be familiar with the industry; it was for that reason that before the first maritime session, in 1920, the International Federation of Seafarers asked that representatives be chosen "amongst recognized seafarers' and shipowners' organizations".[102] On the other hand, the Credentials Committee has at all times considered that a government which consulted a central confederation could not be said to be in violation of the requirements of the Constitution. It did so as a matter of principle in 1926 in a case concerning the United Kingdom Workers' representative.[103] In more recent cases it has appeared to look at the matter more pragmatically.[104] It appears never yet to have been faced with an extreme situation, namely representation exclusively (*i.e.* delegates and advisers) by a central organization without any sectoral affiliate.

More fundamentally, objections have been repeatedly made against Workers' delegates on the ground that there was no freedom of association in their country and that, accordingly, they

[101] Since advisers can be titular members of Committees they can, in fact, play a very active role at the Conference.

[102] Minutes of the Second Session of the Governing Body, p. 39.

[103] Record of Proceedings of the Ninth Session of the Conference, pp. 422ff. It should be noted that, then as now, the National Union of Seamen was affiliated to the T.U.C., and that before (in 1920) and subsequently representation at maritime sessions has been, on the proposal of the T.U.C., by members of the N.U.S. In 1926 (and again in 1929) there may have been personal problems of relations.

[104] See, e.g., Record of Proceedings of the 55th Session of the Conference (1970), pp. 153-4.

could by definition not be representative. A distinction must be made in this connection. In all but one[105] of the cases in which the credentials of Workers' delegates were invalidated, there had recently been suppression of pre-existing workers' organizations. In the sense that structures taken to have been freely established by workers for the representation of their interests were no longer permitted by the State, the absence of freedom of association was considered relevant. On the other hand, in a series of cases in the mid-1950s, international trade union bodies argued that the monolithic trade union organizations in various socialist countries of Eastern Europe and in corporatist Spain could not be considered to be representative because there were limitations on freedom of association in those countries. Without going into the question whether there was indeed no freedom of association, the Credentials Committee of the Conference consistently took the view that, in the absence of evidence that there were more representative bodies (and in the absence of evidence that the existing bodies were not representative), the governments of the countries concerned complied with the constitutional requirements in agreeing on the delegation with the sole existing trade union organization.[106]

As regards employers' representatives the main issue has been whether delegates from countries with wholly socialized economies in fact represent "employers," interests. On the three major occasions on which that question has been considered in the I.L.O. the answer has been that they do so within the meaning of the constitutional requirements. In 1936-7, after the matter had been raised in terms of constitutional principle, the Governing Body took note of an Office report which concluded:

> The qualifications which govern the choice of an employers' delegate may vary at different times and in different places. They are inevitably dependent upon the form of the social regime which exists in a given country.

[105] In the case of South Africa in 1963, the Conference refused to admit the delegate because the only multi-racial trade union organization had not been consulted.

[106] See, e.g., Record of Proceedings of the 37th Session of the Conference (1954), pp. 439ff. It should be noted that the terms of the Constitution provide for the possibility that there may be no "most representative organizations" at all; in such case governments must do their best to find other *indicia* of representativity.

> The worker who benefits by the activities of the International Labour Organization has almost always an employer. No provision requires that this employer should be a private individual ...[107]

In 1945-6, in connection with the reconsideration of the Constitution of the Organization, it was concluded, with the concurrence of "normal" employer representatives, that provision for the representation of socialized management could appropriately be made within the framework of the existing system of representation. Finally, in 1954, the issue of principle was examined by the Credentials Committee of the 37th Session of the Conference.[108] The majority of the Committee — upheld by the Conference — took the view that

> [the] role of the employer must, in its essentials, exist in the structure of any society ... Thus the interests of employers, in any social structure and whatever their relationship to the State, persist and can accordingly be represented in the activities of the International Labour Organization.

The I.L.O. constitutional provision has served as a model for the Arab Labour Organization, a specialized agency of the League of Arab States. Like the I.L.O., the Arab Labour Organization is tripartite. Article 5, paragraph 4, of its Constitution provides for the choice of employers' and workers' representatives at the Conference in agreement with the most representative occupational organizations. The Constitution does not provide for a special procedure to determine compliance with that requirement. However, many of the occupational organizations concerned are familiar with the implementation of the parallel provision in the I.L.O. and it would seem to be legitimate to assume that the principles established in the I.L.O. are taken into account also in the Arab Labour Organization.

On the other hand, the growing acceptance in a number of other organizations — particularly organizations concerned with economic matters — that employers and workers must, as major

[107] Minutes of the 78th Session of the Governing Body (Feb. 1937), pp. 160-2. During the consideration of the report at the following session of the Governing Body, the Director summarized the conclusion as follows: "All those who provided employment for remuneration were employers, and their interests did not coincide with those of the persons whom they employed."

[108] Record of Proceedings, pp. 432-8.

participants in economic life, be associated with their work in some manner, has not been paralleled by legal rules for ensuring the representativity of those so associated, although the various procedures used may in fact result in an appropriate choice.

Article V, section 6, of the Articles of Agreement of the World Bank makes provision for an Advisory Council including representatives of banking, commercial, industrial, labour and agricultural interests. The only guidance to the Board of Governors in selecting these representatives derives from the further provision that the members of the Council representative of fields in which specialized international organizations exist shall be selected in agreement with such organizations. At a meeting in September-October 1946, the Board of Governors decided, as regards the representative of labour, to consult the I.L.O. and the World Federation of Trade Unions (then the sole international trade union federation); on the basis of that consultation it appointed, in 1947, the Workers' Vice-Chairman of the I.L.O. Governing Body.[109]

Article 18 of the Treaty establishing the European Coal and Steel Community provides for a Consultative Committee attached to the High Authority[110] and comprising equal numbers of producers, workers and consumers and dealers. As regards producers and workers, the Article requires the Council to designate representative organizations among which it shall allocate the seats to be filled. The discretion so given to the Council appears to be very wide; it should be recalled, however, that its concerns are limited to two industries.

As regards the European Economic Community, the Treaty of Rome makes provision for two bodies which include non-governmental representatives. In respect of the Economic and Social Committee, Article 193 provides that it shall consist of "representatives of the various categories of economic and social activity, in particular representatives of producers, farmers, carriers, workers, dealers, craftsmen, professional occupations and representatives of the general public". Article 195 further provides that the composition of the Committee shall take account of the need to

[109] See I.L.O., Minutes of the 101st Session of the Governing Body (March 1947), pp. 137-8; 30 I.L.O. *Off. Bull.*, pp. 437-8 (1947). The procedure appears since to have fallen into disuse.

[110] Now the Commission of the merged Communities.

ensure adequate representation of the various categories of economic and social activity. But the Treaty leaves it entirely to the Council, which appoints the Members of the Committee from nominations by Member States, to evaluate their representative character; it may, for that purpose, obtain the opinion of "European bodies which are representative of the various economic and social sectors to which the activities of the Community are of concern". As regards the European Social Fund, Article 124 provides for a Committee composed of representatives of Governments, trade unions and employers' organizations. Again, the Treaty gives no further guidance on the choice of these representatives; Article 127 leaves it to the Council to implement the Treaty provisions concerning the Fund. The main Regulations adopted for that purpose — of 25 August 1960 and 1 February 1971 — also do not deal with the matter.[111] In contrast, when the Council by decision of 14 December 1970[112] established a Standing Committee on Employment composed of representatives of Member States, of the Commission, of employers' organizations and of workers' organizations, it prescribed in meticulous detail which employers' and workers' organizations were to participate; in effect, all major national organizations are represented, mainly through European bodies to which they are affiliated, but in some cases, in the absence of such affiliation, directly.

This brings us to a further aspect of the representation of employers and workers in international organizations, namely representation through bodies established or persons elected at the international level. There are a substantial number of international organizations or associations of employers or workers. Some are general; others are concerned with particular economic sectors. Some are active in a variety of public international organizations; others have been created specifically for relations with a particular organization.[113] Normally their role is advisory only, but they may have additional responsibilities; one example of the latter is their

[111] *Journal officiel 56/60* and *Journal officiel* L. 28/72 — Neither does the Council decision on the Statute of the Committee (*Journal officiel* 56/60 and *Journal officiel* L. 91/68).

[112] *Journal officiel* L. 273/70.

[113] For instance, the business and trade union advisory committees of O.E.C.D. (B.I.A.C. and T.U.A.C.).

involvement, in the I.L.O., in the Council of Europe and in O.E.C. D., in certain procedures concerning the application of standards adopted by the organization. There are no procedures distinct from those, to be considered below, in respect of non-governmental international organizations in general for determining their representativity. However, they stand out from most other non-governmental organizations by features — highly structured, large and well-known national constituents; relatively frequent policy meetings; and high degree of professionalism — which may make this less of a problem in their case.

The election of persons at the international level for the purpose of representing employers and workers in an international organization is probably unique to the International Labour Organization. In particular, the Employer and Worker members of the Governing Body are elected by the Employer and Worker delegates, respectively, to the General Conference; when serving, they are considered to represent, not the employers and workers of their own countries alone, but the totality of employers and workers. The issues regarding electoral systems which are raised by the aim of achieving such wide representativity are known to every constitutional lawyer. At present, to be elected, a candidate must carry a simple majority of the full electoral college. For a long time, it was argued, particularly by minority trade union groups, that a system of proportional representation might produce a more accurately representative result. Detailed consideration of the possibilities in recent years revealed, however, that it was impossible to find a system which would adequately take account both of minority views and of geographical distribution; priority was given to the latter. Accordingly, under proposals elaborated in connection with the review of the structure of the Organization,[114] the majority support of the full electoral college would continue to be required for election, but there would be a regional distribution of seats and candidates would be nominated on the basis of regional consultations, with a minimum support of 20 per cent of delegates from the candidate's region being a condition of eligibility.

[114] See, in particular, Record of Proceedings of the 69th Session of the International Labour Conference (1983), p. 2/12.

4. *International Non-Governmental Organizations (I.N.G.O.s)*[115]

There are hundreds of bodies covered by the title "international non-governmental organizations" which describes, not so much a place in international law, as concern with international matters and, usually, multi-national membership and activities. Many major public international organizations make provision for a variety of consultative relationships with such bodies; these often include the right to attend meetings and to circulate documents. "Consultative arrangements are designed (a) to secure information and advice from organizations having special competence in particular fields, and (b) to enable organizations which represent important elements of public opinion to express their views."[116] It is above all the latter purpose which calls for some reflection on the manner of determining how "important elements of public opinion" may be represented. At the same time, the bodies in question are so varied that issues can be raised only in the most general terms.

First, what is an "important element of public opinion"? The rules of various public international organizations have attempted to answer that question. Resolution 1296(XLIV) of the United Nations Economic and Social Council, on arrangements for consultation with non-governmental organizations,[117] provides that "The organization ... shall represent a substantial proportion, and express the views of major sections of the population or of the organized persons within the particular fields of its competence, covering, where possible, a substantial number of countries in different regions of the world." The W.H.O. Working Principles governing the admission of non-governmental organizations into official relations with W.H.O. similarly specify that

> the organization shall ... represent a substantial proportion of the persons organized for the purpose of participating in the particular field of interest in which it operates. To meet this requirement a group of organizations may form a joint committee or other body authorized to act for the group as a whole.

[115] Other than employers' and workers' organizations.
[116] *Repertory of Practice of United Nations Organs*, vol. III (1955), p. 554.
[117] Adopted in May 1968.

The F.A.O. policy statement concerning relations with I.N.G.O.s refers to organizations "which represent important sections of public opinion"; it also requires, more generally, that I.N.G.O.s be "sufficiently representative". The I.M.O. Rules speak of organizations "representing large groups whose activities have an important and direct bearing on the work of I.M.O.". The U.N.E.S.C.O. Directive provides that membership of I.N.G.O.s with which it establishes relations shall include "a substantial proportion of the groups or persons interested in one or more of the activities falling within U.N.E.S.C.O.'s competence" and shall cover "regular Members in a sufficiently large number and variety of countries to permit it to act, as far as possible, as a valid representative of the different cultural regions of the world". Nevertheless, in a number of organizations the list of I.N.G.O.s with some form of consultative status suggests that quantitative tests are not, in fact, very strictly applied. It would no doubt be difficult to monitor membership claims, initially or on a continuing basis.[118] The value of such tests is in any case open to question. Frequently members of voluntary associations are passive and hence make no genuine contribution to the forming of public opinion. Moreover, measurement of the size of a segment of a population group throws no light on the extent to which that segment can speak for the unrepresented remainder.[119]

Second, how are the views expressed by consultative status bodies evolved? Again, the rules of some public international organizations lay down certain requirements. E.C.O.S.O.C. Resolution 1296 (XLIV) provides that such a body "shall have a democratically adopted constitution ... which shall provide for the determination of policy by a conference, congress or other representative body, and for an executive organ responsible to the policy-making body".

[118] The I.L.O. procedures for admission to consultative status call for information on membership, but there is no question of verification.

[119] For instance, consultative status bodies include a large number of women's organizations. They are loosely assumed to speak on behalf of women. Yet, as the titles of a number of the organizations in question show, many of them are mainly representative of highly educated, professional and no doubt middle class women in developed and semi-developed countries. Their concerns and those of industrial and rural women workers may have little in common. Other organizations, more widely representative at the base, are likely to be effectively represented, again, by professional women.

Elsewhere a "directing body" is required. F.A.O.'s policy statement and U.N.E.S.C.O.'s Directive further provide that an I.N.G.O. shall have procedures and machinery for communicating regularly with its membership. No doubt most I.N.G.O.s comply with these various requirements. Again, however, this reflects only a part of reality. Representative policy-making bodies which may meet only once every four or five years and executive organs which may meet only once a year necessarily leave it to small permanent secretariats or bureaux to evolve the I.N.G.O's position on issues as they arise. Machinery for communicating with Members in different countries has to bridge gulfs of incomprehension. These structural difficulties may be compounded by financial vulnerability: effective participation in the work of a plurality of public international organizations, in different countries, is costly; membership fees must remain at levels which make the I.N.G.O. accessible; and other contributions may accordingly be welcome even if direct or indirect conditions are attached to them. The E.C.O.S.O.C. resolution provides for such contributions to be declared, but it seems to treat as improper only those secretly given by governments as an inducement to undertake acts contrary to the purposes and principles of the Charter.[120] That would not seem to be the main problem.

Third, how does one ensure that the representatives of an I.N.G.O. indeed speak for it? The rules of various public international organizations specify that an I.N.G.O. "shall have authority to speak for its Members through its authorized representatives"[121] or simply that it shall have "authorised representatives";[122] some provide that evidence of the authority may be requested. At the same time, the authority which may be so verified would seem to be essentially formal. Much more rarely there is a provision designed to obtain some assurance that views presented by an I.N.G.O. have genuine representative value: thus, F.A.O. gives an organization in consultative status the faculty to submit written statements on

[120] See para. 36(a), specifying one of the grounds for suspension or withdrawal of consultative status. Para. 36(b), proscribing unsubstantiated or politically motivated acts against Member States, is ambiguous: are such acts in all cases contrary to the Charter, or are they regarded as abusive only if they violate particular principles of the Charter?

[121] E.C.O.S.O.C. Res. 1296(XLIV); W.H.O. Working Principles.

[122] F.A.O. policy statement; U.N.E.S.C.O. Directive.

programme matters, on condition that this is done under the authority of the I.N.G.O's governing body.

Perhaps relatively little attention has been paid hitherto to the genuine representativity of I.N.G.O.s because it was felt not to matter greatly. Such a view may be under-estimating the role played by these bodies, at least in certain contexts. For instance, the questions concerning the circulation of I.N.G.O. communications to the Commission on Human Rights and the relation of such communications to confidential procedures, raised in 1977 by a government and published in the *U.N. Juridical Yearbook* at its request,[123] suggest that the bodies in question play an important part in the "mobilization of shame" which constitutes the main weapon in the implementation of international human rights standards. The pressures for the adoption of international rules on certain aspects of the activities of multinational enterprises, particularly those which led to the W.H.O. text on the marketing of breast-milk substitutes and may lead to standards on the marketing of pharmaceuticals, have come at least in part from I.N.G.O.s.

Questions of the kind outlined here no doubt arise also with respect to pressure groups within States. However, they may be of greater potential importance in public international organizations. It is probably easier to evaluate the real interests of national than of international bodies. It is likely that the members of a national group will be better informed regarding the issues with which it concerns itself than those of an international one. Above all, on the national plane such a group will be working within a highly developed institutional and legal system, whereas on the international plane there is uncertainty as to the proper place of I.N.G.O.s, facilities given to them vary considerably,[124] and there

[123] *U.N.J.Y.B.* 1977, p. 222. See also the procedures on the admissibility of communications adopted by the Sub-commission on the Prevention of Discrimination and the Protection of Minorities in 1971 *A.J.I.L.* 240, 241 (1972): such communications may be submitted by I.N.G.O.s "acting in good faith in accordance with recognised principles of human rights, not resorting to politically motivated stands contrary to the provisions of the Charter of the United Nations and having direct and reliable knowledge of such violations"; not the easiest criteria to verify. On the problems of confidentiality see further E.C.O.S.O.C. Res. 1919 (LVII) of May 1975, and 10 *Netherlands Yearbook* 334 (1979).

[124] For instance, in accordance with its Directive, U.N.E.S.C.O. regularly organizes formal I.N.G.O. Conferences, at which there may be, *inter alia*, a "collective consultation" on U.N.E.S.C.O. programmes.

is some freedom for them to carve out a role for themselves which would require serious justification.

There remains the question whether and to what extent public international organizations require acceptance of their purposes and principles as a condition for the participation in their work of I.N.G.O.s. Some of the rules regarding consultative relations require I.N.G.O.s to have aims and purposes in conformity with the principles of the admitting organization; they do not generally require specific acceptance of these principles.[125] Given the idealistic tone which tends to be given to the statement of the aims of voluntary associations, rules in such terms are not likely to operate as a major criterion of selection. One apparent application, however, merits mention. In the early years of the United Nations, the fact of having legally constituted affiliates in Spain served to exclude an I.N.G.O. from consultative status.[126] More recently, there may be a movement towards a similar approach as regards I.N.G.O.s with affiliates in South Africa.[127] Such an attitude may serve as a potent means of giving effect to relevant United Nations decisions. It is more doubtful whether it establishes valid criteria for determining the aptitude of organizations to contribute to the process of international co-operation.

125 The U.N.E.S.C.O. Directive provides that I.N.G.O.s entering into relations with the Organization shall be "able and willing to make an effective contribution to the achievement of U.N.E.S.C.O.'s objectives in conformity with the principles proclaimed in U.N.E.S.C.O.'s Constitution". The I.M.O. Rules require the objectives and functions of I.N.G.O.s to be "fully in harmony with the spirit, functions and principles" of the I.M.O.

126 See p. 86, note 116 above, at pp. 555-6.

127 See, e.g., E.C.O.S.O.C. Res. 1982/16; Doc. E/1983/11. paras. 137 and 138; Doc. E/1984/29, paras. 8-10; and Doc. E/C.2/1984/D.1. See also Article V of Guidelines on the grant of consultative status adopted by I.M.O. in 1978: "Consultative status shall not be granted to a N.G.O. whose composition or membership are considered to be inconsistent with a decision of the I.M.O. Assembly or Council."

3

The Establishment of Standards of Conduct by International Organizations

The functions of many international organizations include the establishment of standards of conduct for purposes other than the internal functioning of the organization. With the major exception of the European Communities — which are so different that they have to be left out of account here — the organizations in question do not have legislative authority in the sense of having the power to make the standards legally binding on all addressees. The powers of organizations like I.C.A.O., W.H.O. and W.M.O. to make technical regulations,[1] or of organizations like O.E.C.D, or the North-East Atlantic Fisheries Commission to take decisions, come closest to such authority; however, even these powers are accompanied by qualifications — the possibility of refusal by opting out or by notification of inability to comply; the requirement of unanimity; or the recognized need for Members to meet national constitutional requirements before complying — which ensure, in effect, that no State is bound against its will. It is thus appropriate to apply to the entire subject a statement originally made with respect to one of its features, namely that "the great debate of State sovereignty versus world community pervades every aspect of it".[2]

1 For a detailed review of such powers, see K. Skubiszewski, "Enactment of Law by International Organizations", 41 *B.Y.* 198 (1965-1966). See also L. Caflisch, "La pratique Suisse en matière de droit international public", 38 *Ann. Suisse* 1982, p. 69 at 79-88, for an opinion of the Direction du droit international public of the Swiss Federal Department of Foreign Affairs, of March 1981, to the effect that W.H.O.'s regulatory power is strictly limited to non-controversial technical matters which are international in character.

2 J.K. Koh, "Reservations to Multilateral Treaties: How International Legal Doctrine Reflects World Vision", 23 *Harvard Int'l L.J.* 71 (1982).

Currently, the standard-setting function of organizations is seen to be a problem area. That this is so is demonstrated by re-examination of the subject in a number of fora. The General Assembly of the United Nations has, since 1977, undertaken a "review of the multilateral treaty-making process".[3] In the I.L.O. the Director-General made "international labour standards" the main subject of his report to the 70th (1984) Session of the International Labour Conference. U.N.E.S.C.O. examined "The Organization's Normative Action" in 1978,[4] and has pursued review of certain aspects of that action since. In its observations to the United Nations,[5] the Council of Europe indicated that certain aspects of the subject were being considered in the Council. The Institute of International Law has under consideration "L'élaboration des grandes conventions multilaterales et des instruments non conventionnels à fonction ou à vocation normative".[6]

An attempt will be made here to pinpoint some of the main difficulties, with particular reference to their connection with the central subject of our inquiry, namely the adequacy of legal rules governing international organizations. Since one of the issues to be considered is that of the form to be given to standards of conduct, the term "standards" is used in respect both of binding and of non-binding texts.

Standards are directed to many forms of conduct. In particular, while some deal with relations between countries (though not necessarily between governments), others are primarily designed to influence national law and practice in such fields as human

[3] See U.N. Res. 32/48 setting the review in motion; U.N. Doc. A/35/312(1980) for a report of the Secretary-General; U.N. Doc. A/35/312/Add. 2 for comments by the International Law Commission; and U.N. Docs. A/35/312, Add. 1; A/36/553, Add. 1 and 2; and A/37/444, Add. 1 for comments by Governments and other organizations. In 1982 the question was referred to a working group of the Sixth Committee.

[4] See, in particular, Doc. 20C/22 of 25 August 1978.

[5] U.N. Doc. A/36/553, pp. 41-7.

[6] See also the references in F. Morgenstern, "International Legislation at the Crossroads", 49 *B.Y.* 101, 107 (1978), to consideration in the early 1970s of simplified procedures for the amendment of conventional standards, and to consideration of the coordination of the standard-setting activities of different organizations (*ibid.*, at 111-12). General Assembly Res. 37/110 also makes reference to the re-examination of certain aspects of the establishment of multilateral treaties by the Afro-Asian Legal Advisory Committee.

rights, labour, education or health. To some extent the difficulties encountered differ according to whether standards fall into the former or the latter category; in part this is so because the one tends to be static whereas the other is more dynamic in concept. There is, however, too much overlap between the categories, and too much common ground, to make separate treatment feasible. Nor is there any distinctive terminology; however, as regards binding standards, the term "convention" is more frequently used with regard to standards directed to conduct within States, while the term "treaty" is all-embracing.

A. Choice of Subjects for Standards

On the national plane, in democratic societies, the stated policies of political parties, government or opposition, tend to include the framework of legislative programmes. Moreover, different parties are often at one regarding the areas in which legislation is necessary, although they may differ on the specific provisions to be included in the law; certain community needs are readily identified. There are no comparable processes on the international plane. Yet it is increasingly recognized that many of the difficulties encountered in standard-setting, including the limited extent of effective implementation, spring from the decisions to initiate the work leading to standards. The current and recent reviews of standard-setting in various organizations have been examining, *inter alia,* the procedures relating to such decisions. This may not be enough.

1. Origins of Proposals

In most of the organizations engaged in setting standards, proposals for standards on a particular subject mainly come either from the secretariat or from individual or groups of Members, directly or as an offshoot of the consideration in the organization of other subjects. In some organizations such proposals are specifically related to wider programmes. Thus the 1980 report of the Secretary-General of the United Nations on the review of the multilateral treaty-making process noted that U.N.E.P. conceived of the preparation of multilateral, mostly regional agreements

> not as an isolated exercise in treaty-making but rather as an important component in the development of comprehensive and effective action plans, which also involve environmental assessment, environmental management, and institutional and financial arrangements. The result is that the treaty instruments merely provide the legal basis for a cooperative effort to which governments and international organizations have committed themselves.[7]

Elsewhere, and irrespective of whether they are included in a statement having the semblance of a legislative work programme, particular proposals for standard-setting are more *ad hoc* in nature and are not necessarily related either to other aspects of the current work of the organization or to each other.

Each of the two main sources of proposals for standard-setting has drawbacks. Where a particular subject is pressed by some Members of the organization, others are reluctant to oppose, at any rate if no major interests of theirs are prejudiced. The observations of Italy in connection with the U.N. review make the point that "all too often, because of an unwillingness to oppose a rebuttal, negotiations are undertaken without a true perception of their utility".[8] Moreover, expectations are created by an initial readiness to explore a subject which it is difficult to disappoint even if subsequent information casts doubt on the suitability of the subject for standard-setting. Proposals originating with the Secretariat will normally be put forward only after some investigation of their suitability; the problem there lies precisely in the time and resources required for such preliminary work. It is seldom realized that the technical staff of international organizations, which is liable to produce suggestions for standard-setting as an offshoot of research or operational work, is very small. At any one time, that staff can only consider a few areas of possible need in some depth, given also the quantity of information, which may amount to a study of comparative law, to be examined. Accordingly, as the Report of the Director-General to the 1984 International Labour Conference points out, difficulty is experienced in presenting to the representative organs of the organization, for their decision, a sufficient range of subjects which are ripe for action in the sense that the matters to be regulated are clearly defined, that there has been

[7] U.N. Doc. A/35/312, para. 13. [8] U.N. Doc. A/36/553, at p. 27.

adequate technical preparation, and that a sufficient measure of agreement can be secured.[9]

It is widely accepted that the formal preparation of standards should be undertaken only once there is some indication of the feasibility of so doing, on the basis of relevant legal and factual information and an evaluation of need and interest. Only some organizations[10] require both formal decisions to initiate such preparation and feasibility studies to guide the organ taking the decision. However, for the reasons indicated in the preceding paragraph, even these organizations face a dilemma of the "which comes first, the chicken or the egg?" variety. If, as generally required, the decisions are taken after thorough studies have been prepared, the range of options, and hence of priorities, narrows. Conversely, if representative organs make some determination of principle prior to the preparation of feasibility studies, expectations may arise which create a momentum not necessarily conducive to objective later decisions in the light of the studies. There is no ideal solution. Thus both the I.L.O.[11] and U.N.E.S.C.O.[12] have sought in recent years to ensure that Secretariat studies directed to conventions and recommendations are undertaken in the framework of a determination, by representative organs, of the range of questions which might lead to standard-setting. At the same time, in both organizations emphasis has been laid on the need for flexibility both as regards timing[13] and as regards further decisions on feasibility.

2. *Suitability for Standard-Setting*

The question whether a subject lends itself to standard-setting arises mainly, but by no means exclusively, in relation to standards in binding form. The preparation of either binding or non-binding

[9] Report of the Director-General to the 1984 International Labour Conference, p. 18.

[10] In particular I.L.O., U.N.E.S.C.O., Council of Europe, and the Hague Conference on Private International Law.

[11] In the framework of the in-depth review of international labour standards which was undertaken from 1974 to 1979.

[12] See Doc. 20C/22 and Res. 32.1 of the 20th Session of the Conference.

[13] In U.N.E.S.C.O., the Conference, unlike the Director-General, was in favour of defined time-limits for preparatory work.

instruments would seem to be appropriate only where a sufficiently wide measure of agreement can be obtained on rules of conduct which are precise enough to enable the addressees of the rules to understand what is expected of them and to make it possible for the organization to evaluate the extent of effective application. In the case of binding standards, there is the additional issue whether the rules envisaged can be conceived as legal obligations.

These considerations may seem obvious. Nevertheless — perhaps because the means of action available to international organizations are relatively limited — it is not always easy to ensure that they are taken into account in practice. Problems arise, in particular, in three respects.

One is the widespread assumption that all areas of policy are susceptible of being influenced by the enunciation of rules of conduct. In his report to the 1984 Session of the International Labour Conference the Director-General of the I.L.O. suggested that this might not be so:

> Not all the social problems which call for attention by the I.L.O. necessarily lend themselves to standard-setting. Some involve broad questions of policy where standards of a legal nature can play only a secondary role as tools of implementation rather than as determinants of basic approaches. This appears to be the case, for example, as regards rural development programmes and work in certain unorganised sectors. In such circumstances, general discussions aimed at clarifying issues and providing guidance to policy-makers may be preferable to the adoption of Conventions and Recommendations.

As will be further indicated below, there has been argument in the past, in the I.L.O., regarding the suitability of standards, more specifically in binding form, for such fields of action as employment promotion and vocational training. Even as regards non-binding instruments in the form of resolutions, comparison between the Universal Declaration on Human Rights[14] and the Declaration on the Establishment of a New International Economic Order[15] makes evident that the enunciation of principles of conduct lends itself more readily to effective implementation where the legal protection and status of the individual are at issue than as part of the organization of the world economy.

[14] G.A. Res. 217(III). [15] G.A. Res. 3201(S-VI).

A second problem area is that of the limits of recourse to standards purporting to create legal obligations. Although the range of possible instruments is wider, the issue arises in practice mainly as a choice between conventions and recommendations in organizations which have formal and parallel standard-setting procedures for both these types of texts.[16] There is frequently a preference for conventions — in part for the good reason that at present international procedures for the verification of the implementation of an international standard tend to be more thorough and more effective in relation to binding instruments, and in part because of a lack of a clear understanding of the possible uses of different forms of standards. A common result, at least in the I.L.O., is a combination of a convention containing general obligations and a recommendation setting out detailed means of application of these obligations. Frequently the "general obligations" are, in fact, a commitment to pursue stated policy objectives. In a document submitted to the I.L.O. Governing Body in 1974,[17] and echoed in the Director-General's Report to the 1984 Session of the International Labour Conference, the view was taken that

> [t]here can be no doubt of the value of such a legal commitment where the policy objective is defined with precision, and progress in realizing that objective can be evaluated with a fair measure of certainty .... However, where the pursuit of the objectives stated calls for measures over wide areas of public policy, whose relative priority at any given time within over-all government programmes is so much a matter of judgment that evaluation of the extent of compliance with the international commitment becomes hazardous, the use of the Convention form becomes more open to doubt.[18]

A good example of the problem is the I.L.O. Employment Policy Convention, 1964. At the time of its adoption, doubts were expressed by a substantial proportion of Government representatives, on the ground that

> [p]roblems of employment policy are so broad and complex, and the best methods of implementing it are still so uncertain, that a convention could not

[16] But see also the long-delayed choice, in U.N.C.T.A.D. and the United Nations, of the form to be given to standards concerning multinational enterprises.

[17] Doc. G.B. 194/PFA/12/5, para. 49. For government comments on that passage, see Doc. G.B. 198/PFA/11/22, pp. 44-6.

[18] Report of the Director-General to the 1984 International Labour Conference, pp. 15-16.

contain more than a declaration of intentions. The function of conventions, however, was to create specific obligations capable of precise verification.[19]

The Convention is relatively well ratified; the United Kingdom, despite its initial doubts, is a party. In recent years, in the face of soaring unemployment, and government policies giving priority to the reduction of inflation, the supervisory bodies have pressed for continuing attention to the problem of employment and for consultation with employers' and workers' organizations, but have been able to do little more to "enforce" a commitment to promote full employment.

Third, there is the problem of the nature of standards on which it is possible to obtain a sufficient measure of agreement in the membership of the organization. There appear to be subjects with respect to which there is agreement among the membership on certain basic principles but profound divergence regarding the operation of these principles in particular areas of application. A current example is that of international standards regarding the status of women. The United Nations Convention on the Elimination of All Forms of Discrimination against Women, which covers all aspects of their status, including employment, in general terms, has received ratifications at a rate permitting its entry into force within two years. On the other hand, consideration in the I.L.O., with a similar membership, of the revision of older standards specifically protective of women, such as standards prohibiting night work, revealed a total absence of agreement on whether such standards should be abrogated and what, if anything, should be put in their place. If standards are to lay the basis for practical action, it would seem to be desirable to ensure that there exists some consensus, not merely on generalities, but on the types of action to be taken, before the preparation of texts is undertaken.[20] The

[19] Record of Proceedings of the 48th Session of the International Labour Conference (1964), p. 773. See also International Labour Conference, 59th Session, Committee on Human Resources, P.V. 6, p. 12, for legal advice that it was necessary to consider, in relation to a proposed instrument on vocational guidance and training, whether there were elements for a clearly defined and meaningful obligation which could be enforced by the various procedures laid down in the Constitution of the I.L.O.

[20] For comments on the problem of the relation between "umbrella" conventions and more specific texts, see Morgenstern, p. 92, note 6 above, at p. 106.

problem is probably more acute in universal organizations than in regional or sub-regional ones but is not necessarily limited to them.

3. Need and Priorities

One of the major preoccupations at the present time is that the rate of standard-setting, over- all and in particular organizations, is such as to overstrain the capacities of organizations and governments in the preparation of standards, of governments in the implementation of standards and of organizations in verifying their effectiveness. That preoccupation is reflected in many government observations to the United Nations Review of the Multilateral Treaty-Making Process; one government referred to "the international community's unrestrained appetite for new international instruments, which it then has difficulties in digesting nationally".[21] The Secretary-General suggested that one of the questions to be considered in the Review might be whether the international community should seek to reduce the number of treaties being formulated by setting priorities.[22] In U.N.E.S.C.O. the General Conference, in Resolution 6.112 adopted at its nineteenth session in 1976, noted that the preparation of an increasing number of standard setting instruments made it increasingly difficult for Member States to study and give effect to them, and endorsed the view that, "in the field of normative action, quality rather than quantity should be stressed". In the I.L.O. the Report of the Director-General to the 1984 Session of the International Labour Conference stated that it was necessary to consider whether, at least for the time being, a somewhat slower rhythm of standard-setting might not be desirable; the great majority of participants in the Conference discussion of the Report agreed that this was indeed a sound aim.

There is no doubt that one of the factors in the over-production of standards is the plurality of standard-setting bodies and the absence of any single body with an overview of the entire standard-setting process. This dispersion of knowledge and action regarding international standards is, without a doubt, paralleled amongst those responsible for international affairs on the national

[21] Austria. U.N. Doc. A/35/312, Add. 1, p. 2. [22] U.N. Doc. A/35/312, p. 29.

plane. In the United Nations Review of the multilateral treaty-making process, the Secretary-General has posed the question whether the General Assembly should co-ordinate the relevant work of other United Nations organs, of other organizations in the United Nations system and of inter-governmental organizations outside the system. There has been little support for co-ordination, particularly of the work of bodies other than United Nations organs, by reference to the technical specialization and autonomy of those bodies. Some countries — but only some — would be in favour of the General Assembly gathering and disseminating information about treaty-making activities of other organizations. Within the United Nations system, the various Secretariats have sought, for a number of years, to circulate information on such activities to each other, with the more limited aims of avoiding duplication and conflict, and ensuring that statutory provisions on complex technical subjects are established and supervised by those most competent to do so.[23] For a number of good reasons — in particular the absence at this stage of development of the international community of any body with the substantive capacity to evaluate needs in different technical sectors and different regions — and also some bad reasons — governments not being above a little "forum-shopping" — there is little likelihood of more far-reaching concertation of legislative work in the immediate future.

That leaves each standard-setting organization to examine, in its own field of competence, the possibility of establishing priorities amongst potential subjects for standards. A number of constraints

[23] See the annual report for 1973-1974 of the Administrative Committee on Co-ordination to the United Nations Economic and Social Council: Doc. E/5488 of 20 May 1974, paras. 200-8. Even as regards these aims, the 1984 Report of the Director-General to the International Labour Conference points out that "[t]hese arrangements at secretariat level cannot ... ensure that the decisions of policy-making organs will always bring about the best division of work or the most appropriate forms of collaboration among organizations". It cites, as an example, the decision by the General Assembly, in Res. 34/172, to undertake the preparation of a convention on migrant workers, after rejecting proposals to start by analysing existing standards (which include two I.L.O. Conventions) so as to determine on what matters additional standards were needed and in which forum it would be most appropriate to adopt them. For earlier doctrinal consideration of the issue, see C.W. Jenks, "The Conflict of Law-Making Treaties", 30 *B.Y.* 401 (1953), and F. Wolf, "L'interdépendance des conventions internationales du travail", 121 *R.C.A.D.I.* 1967-II, p. 113.

have already been mentioned, in particular the difficulty of obtaining a clear view, simultaneously, both of a reasonably full range of such subjects and of the feasibility of dealing with them. Furthermore, even in organizations with a relatively homogeneous field of competence, Members have been reluctant to establish criteria for priorities. For instance, in the I.L.O. in-depth review of international labour standards which was initiated in 1974, some criteria for the choice of subjects, such as the numbers of workers affected, the potential benefit for economically disadvantaged categories of workers and the severity of the problem, were suggested but were not formally accepted, with a view to avoiding rigidity. In organizations, such as the United Nations, with a much greater diversity of concerns, it would be correspondingly difficult to find criteria having general applicability. A number of States have expressed the opinion, in connection with the U.N. review of the multilateral treaty-making process, that it is not possible to envisage a decision of a general and abstract character to reduce the number of treaties being formulated.[24] Some have gone further: they have emphasized the importance of standard-setting in the international community, of which the proliferation of treaties is merely a reflection, and expressed doubt whether the difficulties being experienced could be met just by reducing the pace of the adoption of texts.[25]

Universal organizations face a problem in determining the need for particular standards, which would not be shared, or would be shared only in attenuated form, by organizations with more limited membership: must projected standards be relevant to the entire membership? Alternatively, should standards of universal application have priority over those of more limited interest? Again, categorical answers would no doubt be dangerous. However, one issue which underlies the question posed is that of the differing priority needs of developed and developing countries respectively. That issue is not the same as that of capacity to comply with advanced requirements, although that capacity may have relevance to

[24] See, e.g., Brazil, U.N. Doc. A/36/553, p. 13; Italy, U.N. Doc. A/36/553, p. 27; Qatar, U.N. Doc. A/37/444, p. 14.

[25] See, e.g., Korea, U.N. Doc. A/37/444, p. 17, and Switzerland, U.N. Doc. A/37/444, p. 19. See also the U.S. emphasis on greater allocation of resources to treaty-making, U.N. Doc. A/35/312, Add. 1, p. 33.

approaches to be followed in standard-setting.[26] The adoption in recent years of certain resolutions in the General Assembly of the United Nations — such as those on permanent sovereignty over natural resources and on the establishment of a new international economic order — and of some binding texts, such as the Code of Conduct for Liner Conferences, in U.N.C.T.A.D., give the impression that the interests of developing countries are now paramount. However, when the standard-setting activities of universal organizations — and particularly those designed to influence national law — are taken as a whole, it may well be that matters which are mainly of concern to these countries are not given sufficient attention and, conversely, that certain subjects which are pursued as technically of universal applicability are of little immediate interest to them.[27] The readier availability of information regarding developed countries, and their continuing greater effectiveness in many fora (related, *inter alia,* to the cost of sending adequate delegations and the availability of specialists for staffing them) makes a balance difficult to achieve. One partial solution is greater recourse to regional instruments; however, in certain fields such fragmentation would defeat the purposes of standard-setting.[28]

There remains what should perhaps be the key question: do international organizations in fact deal with the matters on which standards are of greatest or most urgent importance to the international community? There have been criticisms on the ground, in particular, that organizations are not quick to perceive developing legal problems[29] and are reluctant to venture on to novel ground.

[26] For instance, when in the I.L.O. in 1981 an instrument on workers with family responsibilities superseded an earlier one restricted to women workers, it became clear that the earlier one should have been retained for the guidance of developing countries.

[27] In the 1984 discussion on standards at the International Labour Conference, there was wide agreement that the concerns and values of developing countries were not sufficiently taken into account.

[28] This is true, for instance, of instruments codifying international law. It is also claimed to be true of international labour standards which are intended to set world-wide minima: for a detailed examination of the issue see C. Philip, *Normes internationales du travail: universalisme ou regionalisme?* (1978).

[29] See, for instance, G.L. Morris [D.W. Bowett, "The Impact of the U.N. Structure, including that of the Specialized Agencies, on the Law of International Organization", *Proceedings of the American Society of International Law at its 64th Annual Meeting* 1970, p. 48 at 53] with respect to the problem of the Arctic

In a 1981 study specifically concerned with the International Law Commission, but of potentially wider significance, U.N.I.T.A.R. sought to determine the reasons why the body intended to be at the centre of the progressive development and codification of international law was not at all involved in many of the major legal concerns of the world, such as the law of economic relations, the law of outer space, violence control and human rights;[30] it made certain suggestions, of which some were submitted to States by the Secretary-General of the United Nations in the context of the review of the multilateral treaty-making process, without a conclusive response. Necessarily, the hesitancy or otherwise of organizations to deal with new areas of law is a reflection of the readiness of their Members to undertake — and accept — the regulation of relations and activities which are in a state of evolution; there is no power to enforce legislation desirable for the common weal on a reluctant populace. But there is more: such hesitancy, when compared with the perhaps greater speed of response on the national plane, is also the result of the greater complexity of international standard-setting. Account must be taken of relevant rules of international law, and, in some cases, action must wait on the determination of such relevant rules by other bodies. Account must also be taken of relevant national action. An example which may illustrate these legal inter-relationships with regard to some novel issues is that of proposals, by a number of countries, in the I.L.O., for the regulation of conditions of work on offshore drilling installations. Rules of international law regarding jurisdiction over such installations are relevant, and it was therefore advisable to await the outcome of the — lengthy — negotiations on the law of the sea. A further problem of international law — reminiscent of the early

marine environment: "There is some need to refine and emphasise the allocation of responsibility for continuing study and appraisal of these developing international legal problems."

[30] El Baradei, T.M. Franck and R. Trachtenberg, *The International Law Commission, the Need for a New Direction* (1981). The study identified, *inter alia*, a tendency among members of the Commission to leave progressive development of the law to bodies composed of specifically instructed State representatives; work by consensus leading to concentration on the least controversial issues; insufficiently effective participation of members from developing countries; and insufficient consultation with States Members of the United Nations.

days of the continental shelf[31] — is whether obligations under existing international labour conventions ratified by coastal States cover such installations;[32] it is currently being explored with the States concerned through the supervisory machinery. A complication derived from national approaches lies in the fact that some countries apply their shipping legislation to many of the persons employed offshore while others assimilate them to land-based workers. Against such a background progress is bound to be slow. What may be arguable is that more of the resources applied, both within organizations and within their Members, to questions of lesser importance could on occasion be allocated to resolving the kind of issues which retard an effective response to new, major issues.

B. The Multilateral Treaty

The multilateral treaty has long been considered to be the favourite tool in the standard-setting activities of international organizations. Much has indeed been achieved through its use. With respect to some subjects there exists a network of obligations which has been proudly regarded as the embryo of international legislation.

On the other hand, treaties — even multilateral treaties — are not a means of action specific to organizations. On the contrary, they are one of the traditional sources of international law, subject in the manner of their adoption, operation and termination to rules of international law as developed in inter-State relations. There has been some adaptation of these rules in particular organizations, and such adaptation has been safeguarded by Article 5 of the Vienna Convention on the Law of Treaties. But in relation to the essential feature of a treaty — the creation of legal obligations — the traditional authority of States is unaffected.

[31] See, for instance, the arbitrations on petroleum concessions in Abu Dhabi and Qatar, *Petroleum Development Ltd.* v. *Sheikh of Abu Dhabi*, 18 *I.L.R.* 144, and *Petroleum Development (Qatar) Ltd.* v. *Ruler of Qatar*, 18 *I.L.R.* 161.

[32] See I. Chambers, "The Applicability of International Labour Conventions Offshore: an Approach", 120 *International Labour Review* 395 (1981).

B. The Multilateral Treaty

1. *Ratification, Accession and Other Forms of Acceptance*

Obligations under treaties, conventions, agreements and analogous instruments adopted by or under the auspices of international organizations normally arise from ratification, accession or other forms of acceptance by States. In some cases only Members of the organization concerned can become parties to the instrument; in others accession is open to other States as well. Some of the treaties in question now provide for the possibility of acceptance by international organizations, more or less narrowly defined.

One of the main reasons for current concern about standard-setting is the insufficient total number of ratifications and the slow rate of ratification.[33] To understand the problem some rough figures are necessary. For instance, the membership of the universal organizations is now between 150 and 165. To be binding on just two-thirds of the membership, a treaty must thus have been accepted by 100 States or more. Of the roughly 200 United Nations treaties shown in the volume on the status, as at 31 December 1982, of multilateral treaties deposited with the Secretary-General — some of which admittedly are of exclusive relevance to particular regions — only five[34] had attained that level of support;[35] another dozen or so had been ratified by more than half the membership, while some 30,[36] of which roughly a quarter had been adopted in the preceding four years, were not yet in force. Of over 150 international labour Conventions adopted since 1919 — some of which, again, are by virtue of their subject-matter of interest only to a limited number of States — eight, which include most of the key human rights instruments, have over 100 ratifications, fewer than ten others have been ratified by more than half the membership, while some 20 — of which a third have been adopted in the last four years and another third revised by later Conventions which are in force — are not in effect. The picture in smaller organizations composed of a somewhat more homogeneous

[33] The problem is not new, although awareness of it may be increasing. See, e.g., a 1971 U.N.I.T.A.R. study entitled "Toward Wider Acceptance of U.N. Treaties".

[34] This leaves out of account constitutions of organizations.

[35] They include three texts in which most States have an interest: the Vienna Conventions on diplomatic and consular relations, and the Convention on the Privileges and Immunities of the U.N.

[36] This figure does not include constitutions of organizations.

group of States is not as different as one might expect. Of the hundred-odd conventions adopted by the Council of Europe, over one quarter are shown in the 1981 volume of the European Yearbook to be ratified by two-thirds of the membership; however, twenty-three conventions, of which eight had been adopted in the preceding four years, were not in force.[37] Of the 28 conventions adopted by the Hague Conference on Private International Law, only a couple had been ratified at the end of 1982 by roughly two-thirds of the membership, and three more by half the membership, while eleven conventions — of which five had been adopted in the preceding four years — were not in force.

The rate of ratification is much more variable. It is also difficult to demonstrate by reference to entry into force, given the greatly differing requirements for that purpose. However, it might be recalled that the International Covenants on Human Rights took nearly ten years to enter into force; the Vienna Convention on the Law of Treaties nearly eleven years; and that it will have taken the Code of Conduct of Liner Conferences about fifteen years. It may be that there has been a slowing down of the rate of ratification — an impression gained in comparing the speed of coming into effect of instruments adopted in the 1940s and 1950s with those of conventions adopted in the 1960s and 1970s; this may be due in part to the greater complexity or more esoteric subject-matter of some recent texts. At the same time, it is perfectly possible for treaties which attract the interest of States to come into force very quickly. The International Convention on the Elimination of All Forms of Racial Discrimination, adopted in the same year as the Human Rights Covenants which admittedly cover more ground,[38] came into effect seven years earlier, thanks largely to ratifications by developing countries. The European Convention on the Suppression of Terrorism, adopted in 1977, was in force the following year, although four other conventions adopted by the Council of Europe in that year were not yet in effect by the end of 1981. In the I.L.O., the Merchant Shipping (Minimum Standards) Convention, 1976, despite the sweep of its subject-matter and

[37] Similarly, U.N. instruments which are not in force include a number of regional treaties.

[38] The Covenants also required 35 ratifications as compared with 27 for the Convention; however, by 1969 they had only achieved five or six ratifications.

onerous conditions for entry into force,[39] was effective within five years because of concern with substandard ships.

There is much criticism of the fact that representatives of States vote in favour of treaties which they do not then ratify. Several factors seem to contribute to the disparity; not all of them are deserving of reproach. It is true that delegates in international organizations now[40] tend to support texts which do not prejudice the interests of their country, while their countries will ratify such texts generally only if it is positively in their interest to do so; the gap between negative and positive concerns may be great. However, representatives sometimes deliberately (and expressly) support texts which are of no particular concern to their country in order to enable other countries with a more direct interest in the treaty to bring it into existence. Often delegates will vote for an instrument because they approve of its standards as an aim, even though the implementation of these standards is not within the immediate capacity of their country; the 1984 report of the Director-General to the International Labour Conference regards this as legitimate.[41] The similar attitude of the representatives of countries which may have constitutional difficulties in proceeding to formal ratification may also be justifiable.

Can anything be done to improve the total of ratifications, and hence of legal effect, of multilateral treaties adopted within international organizations? In his report regarding the United Nations review of the multilateral treaty-making process, the Secretary-General made a number of suggestions, ranging from questionnaires designed to ascertain the reasons for non-ratification, through obligations for submission to competent authorities and periodic reports on steps towards ratification, to automatic or provisional entry into force, subject to possible opting out.[42] The

[39] The Convention requires the ratification of States having at least one-quarter of world tonnage, as well as the prior ratification of the key I.M.O. Conventions on safety at sea.

[40] This may be an attitude that has developed over the years.

[41] See Report of the Director-General to the International Labour Conference, p. 12.

[42] Some of these measures were proposed many years earlier for codification treaties. See R. Ago, "La codification du droit international et les problèmes de sa réalisation", *Recueil d'Etudes de droit international en hommage à Paul Guggenheim* (1968), p. 93.

response of States to these various suggestions was not very positive. This is all the more surprising as some of these measures are already in operation in certain organizations. For instance, I.L.O.,[43] U.N.E.S.C.O.,[44] and W.H.O.[45] variously require submission to the competent (usually parliamentary) authority in each Member State — which is designed both to oblige the government to consider appropriate action and to bring the text to public attention — within a specified time from the adoption of a convention, and reports on the steps taken to that end. At the same time the effectiveness of these requirements appears to differ among organizations. In the I.L.O., while only roughly one-third of the membership submits texts to the competent authority within eighteen months from adoption, two-thirds of the membership have usually submitted within five years.[46] On the other hand, in U.N.E.S.C.O., which normally only checks the progress of submission two years after adoption, the rate of submission or at least of reports thereon seems to be much lower.[47] Does the difference lie in the fact that the I.L.O. procedure has been a matter of routine for the ministries concerned for many years, in stricter and more continuous supervision of the procedure by the organization, or in the nature of the instruments at issue? It is difficult to know. At the same time it is more than likely that if a procedure of obligatory submission were applied to all multilateral international instruments adopted within international organizations, the level of compliance with such a procedure would fall.[48] Also, it would appear from the fact that the ratification records of the I.L.O., with an effective system of submission, and of the United Nations, without such a system, are

[43] Constitution, Article 19. [44] Constitution, Articles IV and VIII.

[45] Constitution, Article 20.

[46] See, for instance, the table given in Appendix II to Report III (Part 4A) to the 68th Session of the International Labour Conference (1982).

[47] Indicative figures, which may be as low as 10 per cent of Members, are contained in the various general reports on the initial special reports submitted by Members, adopted at each session of the General Conference. See also a study by the Director-General in Doc. 19C/99.

[48] The observations of the Council of Europe on the U.N. review of the multilateral treaty-making process indicate that a submission procedure was provided for in Res. (51) 30B of May 1951, but that it has never been implemented and is regarded as not being very realistic (U.N. Doc. A/36/553, p. 45).

not dissimilar that the procedure is not a miracle cure for insufficient acceptance of legal obligations.[49]

Non-ratification of a treaty in which a State does not have an urgent interest may be related simply to the burden of national machinery relating to ratification. The burden of national action is greater where compliance with the treaty calls for modification of national law. Accordingly, draftsmen of international conventions specifically designed to set minimum standards for national law in certain fields face a triple dilemma. First, should the convention take maximum account of existing law in Member States, in which case the burden of its acceptance may be reduced but the instrument may represent the lowest common denominator, or should it go beyond existing law at the risk of slow and possibly inadequate acceptance? Second, should the convention contain detail giving substance to the intended principles of conduct but liable to create difficulties in relation to the national law of one country or another, or should it be drafted in more general terms, and hence provide less useful guidance? Finally, to what extent should derogations from the provisions of the instrument be permitted, either by flexibility clauses expressly included therein, or by unilateral reservations by ratifying States?[50]

[49] The procedure may promote practical application where ratification is not possible.

[50] The report of the Director-General of the I.L.O. to the International Labour Conference in 1963 (Report 1 to the 47th Session of the Conference) outlined as follows the desiderata for the drafting of international labour Conventions:

> The terms of Conventions should, unless they deal exclusively with a simple issue of fundamental principle and contain no detail, be sufficiently flexible in character to be susceptible of application under widely varying national conditions . . . A Convention should deal with essentials; it should not contain rigid requirements in regard to matters in respect of which national practice may reasonably vary widely; it should not enter into too much administrative detail; where specific difficulties are known to exist in particular countries or groups of countries when the Convention is under consideration, appropriate exceptions or discretionary powers should be included in the Convention unless a substantial question of principle is involved; in appropriate cases the Convention should permit certain of its provisions to be applied progressively; the scope of the Convention should be so defined that national anomalies of minor importance do not debar or unduly delay ratification. This general approach should not, of course, be carried to the point at which the Convention ceases to be worth having. The balance of advantage may be against including in a Convention some anomalous exception which would permit particular countries to ratify but the international

Derogations, and particularly unilateral derogations, may be regarded as inconsistent with the very notion of an international standard. For this reason, the question whether reservations should be permitted to multilateral treaties has always been a sensitive issue.[51] Some organizations, such as the I.L.O.[52] and the Hague Conference on Private International Law,[53] do not permit unilateral reservations at all. Instead, the standard-setting organ may expressly provide for exemptions, exceptions or variants to meet particular needs: in this manner, the minimum obligation which must be accepted continues to be internationally determined. Some organizations, such as the U.P.U.,[54] require unilateral reservations to be accepted by the legislative organ; this is another way in which the organization, as such, can weigh the compatibility of derogations with the international standard. Yet other organizations, such as the Council of Europe, specify the limited provisions in instruments in respect of which unilateral reservations are permissible. This practice is followed also in some United Nations Conventions; the United Nations Convention on the Law of the Sea does so by the somewhat different method of prohibiting all reservations or exceptions not provided for in individual articles (which may bring it close to the I.L.O. or Hague Conference practice). Even when reservations may be freely made, they frequently do not seriously diminish the effectiveness of the

recognition of which would tend to encourage further countries to adopt it, perhaps unnecessarily. Similarly, a measure of flexibility the result of which is that a large proportion of the Members of the Organisation are not called upon to do more than they are already doing may deprive an international standard of much of its value as a stimulus to further action and achievement ... The problem is one of reconciling these conflicting considerations by weighing and weighting the factors involved as dispassionately as possible in the light of the circumstances of the particular case ... (*Ibid.*, p. 169.)

51 For a detailed examination of the history of reservations to multilateral treaties see J.M. Ruda, "Reservations to Treaties", 146 *R.C.A.D.I.* 1975-III, p. 95. See also Koh, p. 91, note 2 above.

52 See Written Statement of the I.L.O., *Reservations to the Convention on the Prevention and Punishment of the Crime of Genocide, I.C.J. Pleadings*, p. 216, and J.F. McMahon, "The Legislative Techniques of the International Labour Organisation", 41 *B.Y.* 1, 77-85 (1965-1966).

53 Some of the Conventions permit certain so-called reservations. However, these are expressly specified derogations leaving no freedom for unilateral action, and hence are akin to the I.L.O. flexibility clauses.

54 See *U.N.J.Y.B.* 1971, p. 233.

international instrument. For instance, some of the reservations to the Covenants on Human Rights deal with such matters as remuneration for public holidays and the extent of the right to strike in the public service, which are admittedly not world-shaking. Also, when the treaty sets standards of conduct for each State in its own territory rather than for inter-State relations, objections to reservations usually do not result in any diminution of legal relationships. On the other hand, the Vienna Convention on the Law of Treaties has shown that in inter-State relations the combination of reservations and of objections thereto can be far-reaching. In response to reservations bearing on the provisions regarding the settlement of disputes — often, perhaps wrongly, regarded as secondary[55] — a number of States have indicated that they do not consider the substantive provisions which are thus not susceptible of settlement by the prescribed procedures to be in effect as between themselves and the States having made the reservation.[56] Since the Convention at least in part codifies customary international law but the extent to which it does so is not specified, these limitations on its applicability pose serious questions regarding the appropriateness of the multilateral treaty for declaring what the law is.[57]

2. *Revision, Amendment and Abrogation*

The difficulty of making international standards in the form of treaties effective in relation to a substantial proportion of those expected to comply with them is paralleled by the difficulty of modifying or supplementing such standards in the light of relevant changes or of replacing them.

[55] For instance, while ratifications subject to reservations relating to the substantive provisions of the Convention on the Privileges and Immunities of the Specialized Agencies have not been accepted, those with reservations regarding the settlement of disputes have.

[56] The United Kingdom regards the whole Convention as not being in effect in such case. For a detailed examination of the reservations and objections, see J. Sztucki, "Some Questions Arising from Reservations to the Vienna Convention on the Law of Treaties", 20 *German Yearbook* 277 (1977). See also I. Sinclair, *The Vienna Convention on the Law of Treaties* (1973) and D.W. Bowett, "Reservations to Non-restricted Multilateral Treaties", 48 *B.Y* 67 (1976-1977).

[57] These questions were posed in a wider context by K. Marek in "Reflections on Contemporary Law-Making in International Law", *International Relations in a Changing World* (1977), p. 367.

The traditional method of changing a multilateral treaty — and the only one envisaged in the Vienna Convention on the Law of Treaties — consists in the adoption of a new treaty, subject to all the difficulties set out in the preceding section. Accordingly, consideration has been given in many organizations to simplified amendment procedures; generally, such "simplification" is envisaged as bearing, on the one hand, on methods of adoption (agreement between parties without recourse to a conference,[58] or decision by an organ meeting with relative frequency),[59] and, on the other hand, on methods of acceptance (in particular, so-called "tacit acceptance" according to which amendments enter into force for parties to a treaty unless they expressly opt out). It has become evident from such consideration that simplified methods of acceptance will not be applied to modifications of treaty obligations bearing on principles and policies: on the other hand there is interest in and some practice regarding simplified acceptance of modifications of technical provisions of instruments.[60] Even there a great deal of reticence remains: a number of governments, in their observations on the United Nations review of the multilateral treaty-making process, have either refrained from expressing general views, leaving the matter to be considered in each particular case, or have reacted negatively; the Italian comments formulate the underlying conflict in stating that proposals for simplified amendment "seem based on a centralized notion of the international community which is not likely to emerge today".[61]

If there is to be simplified acceptance of modifications to technical provisions, such provisions must be clearly identified. For this reason many existing instances of simplified acceptance procedures regarding amendments to multilateral treaties relate to

[58] See, e.g., Art. 313 of the Convention on the Law of the Sea and the Council of Europe amendment procedure described in U.N. Doc. A/36/553, p. 46.

[59] For instance, the adoption of amendments to certain provisions of I.M.O. Conventions by the Maritime Safety Committee.

[60] In 1972-3 consideration in I.M.C.O. led to the conclusion that amendments to articles of conventions should be subject to express acceptance, but that tacit acceptance procedures might be appropriate for technical annexes. In the current United Nations review of the multilateral treaty-making process, such interest as has been expressed in simplified procedures bears on technical provisions only. For an indication of practice, see above, p. 112.

[61] U.N. Doc. A/36/553, p. 30.

distinct annexes, schedules, regulations and similar formulations. For instance, tacit acceptance procedures, used for many years for the adoption and amendment of the technical annexes to the Chicago Convention on International Civil Aviation, also apply to amendment of the Annexes or Regulations of some I.M.O. Conventions[62] and to amendment of the model forms annexed to the 1980 Convention on International Access to Justice of the Hague Conference on Private International Law; amendments to I.T.U. regulations (but not to the Convention) may be accepted by less formal means than ratification;[63] modifications of the schedules or annexes to some I.L.O. Conventions, while requiring express acceptance by States already parties to the Convention, apply as from their adoption in relation to States subsequently ratifying the Convention;[64] some U.N.E.P. Conventions have technical protocols or annexes which may be amended more easily than the main instrument.[65] In connection with the U.N. review of the multilateral treaty-making process, the idea of framework treaties, defined as treaties whose substantive provisions are set out in separate annexes that may be adopted or changed by an organ established by the treaty or by the organization that promulgated it, commended itself to a number of governments on the understanding that the substantive provisions in question would be technical.

With regard to many of the existing special procedures there is as yet relatively little practice to demonstrate their effectiveness. They may bring problems of their own. Thus, one Government, in its observations for the U.N. review, commented:

> Lately, there has been a tendency to abuse this practice, creating situations of confusion. If treaties are to be properly implemented, States must know what obligations they are assuming. Abuse of simplified forms of amendment, recourse to tacit agreement with reduced time limits, the adoption of amendments in forums other than those which adopted the treaty, the

[62] See, e.g., the Convention on the International Regulations for Preventing Collisions at Sea, 1972.
[63] See, e.g., Article 42(3) of the Torremolinos Convention.
[64] See, e.g., the Migration for Employment Convention (Revised) 1949, and the Employment Injury Convention, 1964.
[65] U.N. Doc. A/35/312, p. 27.

proliferation of amendment proposals (even before the treaty or earlier amendments on the same subject have entered into force) ... can upset the normal process of States' implementation of treaties.[66]

Acceptance is not the only problem area in bringing multilateral treaties up to date under traditional methods; another is the relation of the new to the old. Articles 40 (Amendment of multilateral treaties), 30 (Application of successive treaties relating to the same subject-matter) and 59 (Termination or suspension of the operation of a treaty implied by conclusion of a later treaty) of the Vienna Convention on the Law of Treaties show that the revised and the revising treaties will co-exist unless all parties to the former are also parties to the latter, that States ratifying the revising treaty may remain parties also to the revised treaty and that they may be bound by different rules in relation to other States according to whether these are parties to one or other of these conventions or to both. The practical issues raised thereby relate to the abrogation of treaties and to incompatible obligations.

The chances against all parties to a revised multilateral treaty being parties to the revising treaty are astronomical, particularly if both are open to further ratification.[67] This means that the simple abrogation of such a treaty is virtually impossible, even if it is regarded as being outdated.[68] Consideration of the matter in the I.L.O. in connection with the in-depth review of international labour standards between 1974 and 1977 revealed no procedure which could get over the legal difficulty. The matter is perhaps not of

[66] Spain, U.N. Doc. A/26/553 Add. 1, p. 18. It might also be recalled that the difficulty of revising treaties has sometimes been seen as a safeguard against over-hasty action. And see, G.F. FitzGerald, *The Effectiveness of International Decisions* (S.M. Schwebel, ed., 1971), p. 174, for comments on the inability of States to cope with the frequency of amendments to I.C.A.O. regulatory documents and policy decisions seeking to meet that problem.

[67] International Labour Conventions provide that, on revision, they cease to be open to ratification as from the entry into force of the revising treaty, unless that treaty provides otherwise.

[68] There are degrees in the extent to which treaties lose relevance. For instance, an instrument setting out rules of conduct regarded as inadequate in developed countries may represent an interim goal for developing countries. In the early years of the I.L.O., abrogation of a revised Convention was considered undesirable as a matter of principle, on the ground that it was better for States which did not ratify the revising Convention to remain bound by the old rather than by nothing. The passage of time has somewhat altered that perspective.

overriding importance but it does affect the capacity of the Organization to present to its Members a compact and coherent body of standards, and it may needlessly burden supervisory bodies. The I.L.O. therefore has turned to practical measures to disregard certain obsolete instruments: they are omitted from the published compilation of I.L.O. standards and from the chart of ratifications; it was suggested in the Director-General's Report to the 1984 Session of the Conference that consideration might also be given to discontinuance of detailed reporting on some Conventions.[69]

The fact that States may be bound by incompatible obligations under a revised and a revising treaty appears to be a matter of concern to some of the countries which have submitted observations in connection with the U.N. review of the multilateral treaty-making process.[70] Where the earlier instrument can be denounced in connection with acceptance of the later, the problem does not arise. However, the freedom given to States to withdraw from their obligations under multilateral treaties affects the stability of international standards; frequently, therefore, treaties can only be denounced after a specified initial period[71] or at specified intervals, usually of five or ten years.[72] International labour Conventions have since 1929 specifically provided that ratification of a revising Convention will *ipso facto* involve the immediate denunciation of the revised Convention, as from the entry into force of the revising Convention; that system — which balances the need for stability and that for tidy modification — does not appear to be used in other organizations

3. Legal Relationships Created by Treaty

Treaties create legal obligations for parties to them; overwhelmingly these parties are States. Frequently, however, the rules of

[69] See the Director-General's Report to the 1984 Session of the International Labour Conference, p. 14.

[70] See, e.g., the Netherlands, U.N. Doc. A/36/553/Add. 1, p. 11, and Australia, U.N. Doc. A/37/444, p. 10.

[71] See, e.g., the European Convention on Human Rights. The U.N. Covenants on Human Rights do not provide for denunciation at all.

[72] See, e.g., the Genocide Convention, international labour Conventions, conventions adopted by the Hague Conference on Private International Law and the European Social Charter.

conduct laid down by international organizations are directed towards the activities of individuals, companies or associations within States. As the law stands at present, it is not normally possible for these natural or legal persons to be directly bound by legal provision prescribed by international organizations in the form of multilateral treaties.[73] Accordingly, treaties are likely to be so drafted as to require States to prescribe the appropriate rules of conduct and to have appropriate systems of enforcement. In turn, international supervisory machinery must declare itself satisfied where there are adequate procedures to obtain compliance; it cannot judge the result. For instance, in one of the rare cases in which a complaint was made under the I.L.O. freedom of association procedures on the ground of the actions of the employing company and not of the State, the Governing Body Freedom of Association Committee addressed itself to the questions whether occupational organizations were provided by national law with the means to enforce their rights and whether there had been a denial of justice in the failure of the Government itself to initiate court action.[74] During preparatory work, again in the I.L.O., on international standards for multinational enterprises some thought was given to the possibility of acceptance by these enterprises of the terms of a convention,[75] perhaps in a manner analogous to the acceptance by international organizations of obligations under international treaties to which they are not formally parties: the idea was rejected as being impracticable.

Legal obligations under treaties adopted by or under the auspices of international organizations thus lie only on States — but in relation to whom? Traditionally (and logically, if treaties are seen as contracts) obligations are accepted exclusively in relation to

[73] Under self-executing treaties it may be possible for such persons to have direct rights. However, both because of differing methods of incorporating treaties in national law, and because international standards often require to be supplemented by rules regarding their application, the self-execution of multilateral treaties does not play a great role in practice. See, e.g., N. Valticos, "Conventions internationales du travail et droit interne", 41 *Rev. crit.* 251 (1955).

[74] Fifty-second report, paras. 166-76, 44 I.L.O. *Off. Bull.* 255-7 (1961). See also A.A. Cancado Trindade, "Exhaustion of Local Remedies under the U.N. Covenant on Civil and Political Rights and its Optional Protocol", 28 *I.C.L.Q.* 734 (1979).

[75] The idea was again put forward by the representative of Canada at the 1984 Session of the International Labour Conference (P.R. 31/4-6).

other States which have similarly accepted. The concept that States parties to a multilateral treaty, even if it is not contractual, are solely concerned thereby remains widespread. For instance, when the Committee established under Article 8 of the U.N. Convention on the Elimination of All Forms of Racial Discrimination to supervise its implementation concluded, unanimously, that a reservation to the Convention which had been accepted by the parties was incompatible with the object and purpose of the Convention and sought legal advice regarding the effect of its decision, the United Nations Secretariat advised that the decision had no legal effect, on the ground that "the Committee is not a representative organ of the States parties (which alone have general competence with regard to the implementation of the Convention)".[76] It would seem, nevertheless, that in certain circumstances and subject to certain safeguards obligations exist in relation to the organization as well.

Where the Constitution of an organization provides — as is the case with the I.L.O., U.N.E.S.C.O. or W.H.O. — for the setting of standards in the form of treaties, and particularly where it establishes an enforcement procedure under which the reports of States on the application of a ratified treaty are examined by organs of the organization or bodies established by it, the organization would seem to be given a legal interest in the performance of obligations under the treaty. The same may be true where enforcement machinery is established under the terms of a particular convention — such as the European Social Charter — as long as the supervisory body indeed acts for the organization. On the other hand, where, as in the case of the Human Rights Committee established under the United Nations Covenant on Civil and Political Rights,[77] or the supervisory committees established under the Conventions on the Elimination of All Forms of Racial Discrimination and Discrimination against Women, the body is elected by States parties to the treaty from amongst their nationals, there may be some collectivization of the interests of these parties, but the role of the organization is reduced to lending appropriate assistance.

[76] *U.N.J.Y.B.* 1976, p. 220 at 221.
[77] Reports on the implementation of the Covenant on Economic, Social and Cultural Rights go to the U.N. Economic and Social Council.

Complaint procedures also show a variety of patterns. Where inter-State complaints are provided for, either in the Constitution of an organization or in a specific treaty adopted by it, they are usually restricted to States parties to the treaty the implementation of which is at issue.[78] This reflects traditional attitudes, although it may also be designed to prevent misuse of the bodies established to consider complaints, for political purposes, by States which do not have relevant obligations. Complaints[79] by individuals or non-governmental organizations are of two main kinds. Under human rights conventions the standing to submit them tends to be limited to persons or bodies claiming to be a victim of a violation. They derive a procedural right from the treaty and may benefit from the outcome of the procedure. It is nevertheless doubtful whether they have a direct legal interest in the substantive provisions of the treaty; certainly a formal decision[80] of the body examining their complaint is not immediately effective in the State concerned. On the other hand, their procedural right enables the body empowered to deal with the complaints and, where that body is established by the standard-setting organization, through it the organization to concern itself with the implementation of the substantive obligations. The second type of procedure goes further. Under Articles 24 and 26 of the I.L.O. Constitution non-governmental organizations and delegates to the Conference can set in motion procedures for the investigation of alleged non-compliance with obligations under international labour Conventions even though they are not themselves affected by the violation;[81] the procedures can also be initiated by the I.L.O. Governing Body. These persons and bodies thus represent a community interest in the performance of the obligations in question.[82] Limitations remain because of the pattern of other aspects of international law. Thus, although one and the same

[78] See, e.g., I.L.O. Constitution, Article 26, para. 1; U.N. Covenant on Civil and Political Rights, Article 41; European Convention for the Protection of Human Rights and Fundamental Freedoms, Article 24 and Article 44.

[79] Whatever may be their formal description — petition, communication, representation, etc.

[80] There are procedures falling short of decision; for instance the European Commission of Human Rights has the power to effect "a friendly settlement".

[81] Non-governmental organizations have an analogous standing under the special procedures relating to freedom of association.

[82] For a well-known affirmation of this interest, see the opinion of Judge Jessup in the *South-West Africa Cases, (Ethiopia* v. *South Africa; Liberia* v. *South Africa),*

procedure applies to inter-State complaints and to complaints initiated by delegates to the Conference or by the Governing Body of its own motion, a possible final step open to a complaining State, namely that of referring the complaint to the International Court of Justice for final decision, is not open to the organization.

Finally, there are some features in the application of general treaty law in certain organizations which tend to suggest that standards established by these organizations are not the sole property of ratifying States. For instance, the development in the I.L.O. of a constitutional practice according to which international labour conventions may not be ratified with reservations was based in part on the consideration that these conventions were adopted by an organ in which representatives of employers and workers, as well as of governments, participated and that governments alone were thus not free to vary their terms. Analogous reasoning may apply to the proposition, referred to in Chapter I, that States parties to a treaty regulating conduct within their territories rather than their mutual relations cannot modify their obligations by *inter se* agreement. It may be contrary to the object and purpose of the treaty in the terms of the Vienna Convention to do so — it is after all unthinkable that a State having committed itself to proscribe slavery, forced labour or torture should be able to go back on that commitment in such a manner; at the same time, is the "object and purpose" of the treaty not a reflection of the concerns of a wider community? And if the question is then pondered whether the commitment could be defeated by the joint decision of all the States having ratified the treaty, the conclusion may be that the wider community is the one which established the standards, not the group of States which are up to that moment formally committed to them. The further issue of the effect of hostilities on standards established by an international organization and involving some inter-State relations is also illuminating. While the practice of organizations, like the Vienna Convention with respect to treaties in general, does not provide a conclusive answer to the substance of the question, both I.L.O.[83] and

Preliminary Objections, I.C.J. Reports 1962, p. 316; 37 *I.L.R.* 3; Second Phase, *I.C.J. Reports* 1966, p. 6; 37 *I.L.R.* 243.

[83] See, in particular, Minutes of the 95th Session of the Governing Body (June 1945), pp. 164-6 and Record of Proceedings of the 27th Session of the International Labour Conference (1945), pp. 439-40. In a national Court decision, the Court of Appeal of Aix, France, held in 1951 in *Etablissement Cornet*

I.C.A.O.[84] have made it clear that the appropriateness of a suspension of their obligations cannot be finally determined by the States concerned but is subject to review by an international body.

C. Non-Binding Standards

Some of the shortcomings of multilateral treaties as vehicles for the setting of international rules of conduct — in particular, the low average proportion of intended addressees bound by them, delays in their coming into effect, and the potentially quirky result of the interplay of such factors as individual acceptances, reservations and objections thereto and the co-existence of revised and revising texts — may have served to focus attention on alternative forms of action exempt from these difficulties. There is nothing new about the use of non-binding instruments for setting international standards, although it is possible that in certain contexts they have assumed greater importance recently. What is relatively new is the widespread concern with the question whether non-binding instruments can have law-creating effects and, if so, in what manner.[85]

It is not proposed to duplicate or even summarize here the substantial literature on the legal effects of resolutions of the General Assembly of the United Nations[86] or of non-binding codes of conduct

v. *Gaido*, 38 *Rev. crit.* 697 (1952), that ratification of an I.L.O. Convention regarding the application by a ratifying State of workmen's compensation legislation to the nationals of other ratifying States was tantamount to "affiliation" to an international system and that the obligations assumed in relation to the organization were not brought to an end by war, although the exercise of rights thereunder might have been suspended during hostilities.

84 See *Appeal Relating to the Jurisdiction of the I.C.A.O. Council (India* v. *Pakistan), I.C.J. Reports* 1972, p. 46; 48 *I.L.R.* 331.

85 On the general question, see, e.g., O. Schachter, "The Twilight Existence of Non-Binding International Agreements", 71 *A.J.I.L.* 296 (1977); R.R. Baxter, "International Law in 'Her Infinite Variety'", 29 *I.C.L.Q.* 549 (1980); M. Bothe, "Legal and Non-Legal Norms — A Meaningful Distinction in International Relations?", 11 *Netherlands Yearbook* 65 (1980).

86 See, e.g., H. Golsong, "Das Problem der Rechtsetzung durch internationale Organisationen", *Berichte der Deutschen Gesellschaft für Völkerrecht*, Vol. 10, (1971); G. Arangio-Ruiz, "The Normative Role of the General Assembly of the U.N. and the Declaration of Principles of Friendly Relations", 137 *R.C.A.D.I.* 1972-III, p. 419; R. Higgins, "The U.N. and Lawmaking, the Political Organs", *Proceedings of the American Society of International Law* 1970, p. 37; S. Schwebel, "The Effect of Resolutions of the U.N. General Assembly on Customary International Law", *Proceedings of the American Society of International Law* 1979,

for multinational enterprises.[87] Nor are the questions whether such instruments can reflect, restate or create customary international law or general principles of law, or indeed constitute a new source of law, which remain highly controversial, of immediate practical relevance in the work of organizations. Accordingly, it is proposed to consider here only two matters which do have such relevance: first, the types of non-binding instruments which are available to and used by organizations and the purposes for which they may be used; and, second, the methods open to and used by organizations to promote the effective application of these instruments.

1. Types of Non-Binding Instruments

The only non-binding instrument provided for in the constitutions of various organizations[88] for the specific purpose of standard-setting is the Recommendation.[89] Typically, it is there referred to in conjunction with provisions for conventions, agreements and other forms of binding standards. Its purpose may be analogous: to serve as the basis for national action to give legal effect to its substance. For instance, the U.N.E.S.C.O. Rules of Procedure concerning Recommendations to Member States and International Conventions Covered by the Terms of Article IV, Paragraph 4, of the Constitution refer, in Article 1, to

> Recommendations in which the General Conference formulates principles and norms for the international regulation of any particular question and invites Member States to take whatever legislative or other steps

p. 301; M. von Grüningen, "Die Resolutionen der Generalversammlung der Vereinten Nationen und ihr Einfluss auf die Fortbildung des Völkerrechts", *Festschrift für R. Bindschedler* (1980) p. 187.

87 See, e.g., Hans W. Baade, Ian Brownlie and A.A. Fatouros, *Legal Problems of Codes of Conduct for Multinational Enterprises* (Norbert Horn, ed. 1980).

88 See, in particular, Article 19 of the I.L.O. Constitution; Article IV(3) of the F.A.O. Constitution; Article IV(4) of the U.N.E.S.C.O. Constitution; Article 23 of the W.H.O. Constitution; Article 37 of the Chicago Convention on International Civil Aviation; Article 3(a) of the I.M.O. Convention; Article 15 (b) of the Statute of the Council of Europe.

89 The word "recommends" may be found in a variety of non-binding instruments. In the classification which is attempted here, the term "Recommendation" is used only for instruments having a certain formal status under the various Constitutions; frequently (e.g. I.L.O., F.A.O., I.C.A.O. and Council of Europe) they require a qualified majority for adoption.

may be required — in conformity with the constitutional practice of each State and the nature of the question under consideration — to apply the principles and norms aforesaid within their respective territories.

Similarly, Article 19, paragraph 6, of the I.L.O. Constitution provides that a Recommendation "will be communicated to all Members for their consideration with a view to effect being given to it by national legislation or otherwise". A more comprehensive statement of the possible role of Recommendations was made by the Delegation on Constitutional Questions of the International Labour Conference which reviewed the I.L.O. Constitution in 1946:

Recommendations, like Conventions, are designed ... to fulfil a variety of purposes. In some cases the principal objective of a Recommendation is the creation of a measure of international uniformity as regards matters in respect of which such uniformity is desirable; the promotion of such uniformity by a Recommendation may facilitate the acceptance at a later date of international obligations where such are desirable, and in other cases may make the acceptance of such obligations for the purpose of ensuring uniformity unnecessary, and thus secure some of the advantages of the existence of a network of obligations, while preserving greater freedom of national action. In some cases a Recommendation is primarily a contribution to the creation of a common social consciousness extending beyond frontiers ... Frequently the main function of a Recommendation is to contribute to the wise handling of social and labour problems by the formulation in an authoritative manner of standards or principles which embody conclusions drawn from the experience of a large number of countries, supplemented by research into new problems and a careful evaluation of new aspirations and the practicability of giving effect to them ...[90]

Recommendations are designed to be used instead of binding standards, according to the nature of the activities of the Organization, for subjects which "owing to their complexity and the wide differences in the circumstances of different countries, will be incapable of being reduced to any universal and uniform mode of application",[91] for technical matters in respect of which action is desirable but not essential[92] or for specifying standards which are

[90] International Labour Conference, 29th Session (1946), Report II(1), pp. 37-8.

[91] Report of the Commission on International Labour Legislation of the 1919 Peace Conference, 1 I.L.O. *Off. Bull.* 264 (1919-20).

[92] I.C.A.O. definition, followed in I.M.O. (with respect to the Facilitation Convention) and in W.H.O.

too novel, too advanced or too detailed for inclusion in binding texts. The extent to which and the manner in which they are in fact used varies as between organizations as well as over time. For instance, a substantial part of U.N.E.S.C.O.'s relatively large body of standards takes the form of Recommendations alone. On the other hand, in the I.L.O., Recommendations have been used in recent years mainly to supplement, in more detail, Conventions on the same subject adopted at the same time. In his report to the 1984 Session of the International Labour Conference the Director-General pointed out that this was tantamount to using them as second-class instruments and suggested that there were other possibilities:

> In earlier times many subjects were dealt with in Recommendations, particularly where matters of general policy or practical programmes were involved or where, in the absence of sufficient development of national experience, standards of an exploratory character appeared to be called for. That approach is now rare.

That decline of the Recommendation is a reflection of the importance attached to conventions and the recourse to "promotional" conventions and other texts the obligations of which are set forth only in the most general terms. From the point of view of the balanced development of the law it is regrettable.[93]

A second type of non-binding instrument consists in detailed models for national laws, regulations and codes of practice. For instance, the International Labour Office has produced and revises from time to time, with the assistance of *ad hoc* expert meetings, a number of publications containing detailed specifications bearing

[93] As early as 1945 the Director of the International Labour Office wrote:

> Any attempt to enhance the authority of what is in substance a Recommendation by expressing it in Convention form in the hope of securing for it such additional prestige as may attach to Conventions would seem to be calculated to undermine the authority of Conventions and Recommendations alike. It obscures the true character of Conventions as instruments one of the essential purposes of which is the creation of obligations, and tends to discredit the Convention technique by resulting in widespread failure to ratify, and it equally tends to discredit the Recommendation by gratuitously implying that because a Recommendation is not an instrument for the creation of obligations it is therefore ineffective as an instrument designed to influence policy and legislation by the definition of an international standard. (Director's Report to the 27th Session of the International Labour Conference, pp. 155-6.)

on occupational safety and health in different industries and occupations. W.H.O. has established, again on the basis of the work of expert groups, directives on the designation and supervision of pharmaceuticals. F.A.O. experts have adopted standards concerning the designation, definition and composition of milk and milk products. The three organizations jointly have worked on standards regarding pesticides. F.A.O. and W.H.O. have complex joint machinery for the elaboration of food standards — the *Codex Alimentarius* — including provision for the acceptance of such standards by governments.[94] I.A.E.A. has established safety standards for radiation protection. A harmonization of national laws and practices is aimed at by instruments of this kind, for the benefit, on the one hand, of workers and consumers and, on the other, of the movement between countries of goods and services.

Finally, there are resolutions (whatever may be the name given to them on particular occasions). Not all resolutions lay down rules of conduct; however, an important minority do. In essence, these contain statements of policy. When it is desired to give such a statement particular solemnity the resolution may be called a "Declaration".[95] The degree of real commitment to the policies so enunciated may vary. In some cases it is strong: for instance, the seriousness with which the International Labour Conference in 1944 adopted a Declaration on the Aims and Purposes of the Organization was demonstrated by the fact that two years later it was embodied in the Constitution. In other cases a Declaration acquires impetus over time: the authors of the Universal Declaration of Human Rights may have been a group of cynics,[96] but 35 years later half of a greatly expanded membership of the United Nations was bound by legal provisions largely based on it. Indeed, a number of U.N. Declarations have been forerunners of presently existing or currently proposed standards in treaty form;[97]

[94] See, in particular, J.P. Dobbert, "Le Codex Alimentarius, vers une nouvelle méthode de réglementation internationale", 15 *Ann. Français* 1969, p. 677.

[95] As in the case of Conventions, it may be that there is a tendency to make use of Declarations in circumstances which do not warrant this.

[96] See H. Lauterpacht. "The Universal Declaration of Human Rights", 25 *B.Y.* 354 (1948).

[97] Declaration on the Elimination of All Forms of Racial Discrimination (G.A. Res. 1904(XVIII)); Declaration on the Elimination of Discrimination Against Women (G.A. Res. 2263(XXII)); Declaration on the Rights of the Child (G.A.

the purpose of having recourse to Declarations in the first instance has been stated by the Secretary-General of the United Nations to be, on the one hand, "to ameliorate the situation to which it is addressed more quickly than by means of or pending the completion of a long-range treaty-making project" and, on the other, to "constitute a guideline for such a project or assist in testing in practice certain principles before they are firmly embodied in a treaty".[98]

Amongst objections sometimes made to resolutions as standard-setting instruments is that they can be adopted without the degree of preparation given to more formal texts and without the degree of support frequently required for the latter. At the same time, some such texts are very carefully prepared and negotiated and enjoy general support. All the existing Codes of Conduct for Multinational Enterprises[99] are instruments of this kind: the O.E.C.D. Declaration on International Investment and Multinational Enterprises, with attached Guidelines; the I.L.O. Tripartite Declaration on Multinational Enterprises and Social Policy; and the U.N.C.T.A.D. Set of Multilaterally Agreed Equitable Principles and Rules for the Control of Restrictive Business Practices. Their adoption as resolutions epitomizes the advantages which this form of action may have in certain circumstances over treaties: many aspects of the subject are new and rules need to be flexible and readily adaptable; the rules are addressed as much to the enterprises as to States; and, insofar as action by States is called for, there is a need for international co-operation through such a network of relations that the normal method of entry into force of treaty obligations could delay the effective implementation of the rules beyond all reasonable expectation.

Res. 1386(XIV)); Declaration on the Protection of all Persons from being Subjected to Torture (G.A. Res. 3452(XXX)); Declaration of Principles Governing the Sea-Bed and the Ocean Floor, and the Subsoil Thereof, beyond the Limits of National Jurisdiction (G.A. Res. 2749(XXV)).

98 U.N. Doc. A/35/312, para. 29, p. 16. Declarations may thus be used in the United Nations in a manner analogous to that of Recommendations elsewhere.

99 The W.H.O. International Code on the Marketing of Breast-Milk Substitutes, which is sometimes regarded as falling into this category, is a Recommendation under Article 23 of the W.H.O. Constitution.

2. *Implementation of Non-Binding Instruments*

In a recent spirited attack on theories which obscure the distinction between binding and non-binding standards,[100] the author points out that a cardinal feature of the former, which is not shared by the latter, is that they can be relied on before a Court and can lead to international responsibility. However, with rare exceptions,[101] international organizations do not rely on judicial action for the enforcement of their standards in the form of multilateral treaties, and it is unusual for these to give rise to State responsibility in the classical sense. The methods mainly used for the implementation of binding standards are two-fold: on the one hand, the objective determination of the degree of compliance, accompanied by a certain publicity for serious violations — what has become known as the "mobilization of shame"; on the other, assistance, mainly through advisory services, in securing the full implementation of the standards.[102]

There is nothing inherently unsuitable in methods of this kind for the promotion of non-binding standards. Some adaptation may be necessary: thus it is difficult to speak of "violations" of a standard in respect of which no obligations have been assumed.[103] But assistance, fact-finding, evaluation of the degree and manner of implementation, and even procedures for the settlement of

[100] P. Weil, "Towards Relative Normativity in International Law?", 77 *A.J.I.L.*, 413 (1983).

[101] Such as the European Convention on Human Rights. In some cases judicial settlement is envisaged in basic texts but is not used in practice. Thus the provision of Article 37 of the I.L.O. Constitution, to the effect that any dispute relating to the interpretation of a Convention concluded in pursuance of its terms shall be referred to the International Court of Justice, has never been invoked, although there were some requests for Advisory Opinions in the early years of the Organization. Similarly, the findings of a Commission of Inquiry on an inter-State complaint have never been referred to the Court under Article 29 of the Constitution.

[102] For a description of methods of application of binding international standards, which are not further discussed here, see, e.g., N. Valticos, "Un Système de controle international: la mise en oeuvre des conventions internationales du travail", 123 *R.C.A.D.I.* 1968-I, p. 311.

[103] But see the individual opinion of Sir Hersch Lauterpacht in the *South-West Africa — Voting Procedure* case, to the effect that, while States are not bound to accept recommendations of the General Assembly, they are bound to give them due consideration in good faith and to explain the reason for a decision to disregard them. (*I.C.J. Reports* 1955, p. 67 at 118-20; 22 *I.L.R.* 651 at 684-7.)

disputes regarding the meaning and scope of the standards can be and are used for the purpose of giving effect to non-binding instruments.

Where the constitutions of organizations make provision for recommendations as well as for conventions or other binding standards, the same or similar procedures for supervision (although not for complaints) may apply. Thus in I.L.O. and U.N.E.S.C.O. requirements for the submission of standards adopted by the Conference and for reports on such submission apply to conventions and recommendations alike. Also, in I.L.O., U.N.E.S.C.O. and W.H.O. reports on the effects given to the instruments are envisaged for both. In W.H.O. these are annual for either type of instrument. In the I.L.O. reports on ratified Conventions are called for and examined by the supervisory organs more frequently and regularly than those on Recommendations (or unratified Conventions). This is one reason for the preference often given to Conventions, even though these may be drafted in general terms, particularly as the supervisory bodies may derive guidance from Recommendations supplementing the Conventions in determining the nature of the obligations arising thereunder. The Statute of the Council of Europe gives the Committee of Ministers the authority to request the Governments of Members to inform it of the action taken by them with regard to Recommendations.

The advantage of such constitutional provisions is that, although the standards to which they refer are not binding, the procedures directed towards their application are. Nevertheless, in the absence of such provisions arrangements have been made from time to time, either through decision of an organ of the Organization or through the terms of a particular Recommendation, to establish analogous procedures or to supplement existing ones. For instance, there are no obligations with respect to Recommendations made by the General Assembly of the United Nations under Article 13(1)(b) of the Charter.[104] However, in the 1965 Recommendation on Consent to Marriage, Minimum Age for Marriage and the

[104] Article 64 of the Charter empowers the Economic and Social Council to make arrangements with the Members of the United Nations to obtain reports on the steps taken to give effect to recommendations on matters falling within its competence made by the General Assembly.

Registration of Marriages,[105] the Assembly "recommended" that the Recommendation be submitted to the competent authorities for the enactment of legislation or other action within eighteen months, that Member States inform the Secretary-General of the action taken and that Member States further report at five-yearly intervals on the law and practice in their countries regarding the matters dealt with in the Recommendation, showing the extent to which effect has been given or is proposed to be given to the provisions of the Recommendation; these procedures, which are based on those of the I.L.O. Constitution, parallel provisions of the United Nations Convention on the same subject. The various reports are to be examined by the Commission on the Status of Women. Again, in respect of the 1966 Recommendation on the Status of Teachers, prepared jointly by U.N.E.S.C.O. and I.L.O. and adopted by a conference outside the constitutional framework of either organization, there are supervisory arrangements which were decided by parallel action of the U.N.E.S.C.O. Executive Board and the I.L.O. Governing Body, and which provide for five-yearly reports and their examination by a Committee of independent experts jointly appointed by the two organizations and reporting to both. The W.H.O. Code on the marketing of breast-milk substitutes supplements the constitutional reporting provisions by requiring the Director-General to submit reports on the status of implementation of the Code to the World Health Assembly every other year and to give technical support to Member States preparing national legislation or taking other measures in implementation and furtherance of the Code.

Recommendations can be addressed to persons or entities other than States. The W.H.O. Code contains provisions which seek, in an original manner, to obtain the participation of such persons or entities in implementation or monitoring. Under Article 11.2 manufacturers and distributors of products within the scope of the Code and appropriate non-governmental organizations, professional groups and consumer organizations are to collaborate with governments in monitoring the application of the Code; this type of role is given them elsewhere also.[106] Under Article 11.3

[105] Adopted by G.A. Res. 2018(XX).

[106] For instance, under the I.L.O. Constitution employers' and workers' organizations must receive copies of all government reports on the submission and

manufacturers and distributors of products within the scope of the Code "should regard themselves as responsible for monitoring their marketing practices according to the principles and aims of this Code, and for taking steps to ensure that their conduct at every level conforms to them"; they are also expected, under Article 11.5, "to apprise each member of their marketing personnel of the Code and of their responsibilities under it". Most novel is the provision of Article 11.4 according to which non-governmental organizations, professional groups, institutions and individuals concerned "should have the responsibility of drawing the attention of manufacturers or distributors to activities which are incompatible with the principles and aims of this Code, so that appropriate action can be taken"; the governmental authority concerned is also to be informed. The most recent report to the World Health Assembly on the operation of the Code[107] indicates that a number of non-governmental organizations have kept W.H.O. informed of their activities in pursuance of that paragraph.

There are usually no procedures for the supervision of the implementation of non-binding standards in the form of model laws or codes of practice.[108] The gap is likely to be related to the nature of the standards in question, but it is a matter for speculation what particularity is determining. Some standards of this kind, such as the I.L.O. ones, are not examined by representative bodies; others, such as the *Codex Alimentarius* ones, are. All the standards in question are highly technical and deal with detail rather than with issues of general policy. In some cases they are supplementary to more

application of Conventions and Recommendations and can make comments thereon both to the government and directly to the Organization. The Tripartite Consultation (International Labour Standards) Convention, 1976, which has been ratified by roughly one quarter of the membership, provides further for procedures under which there will be consultations on the proposals to be made to the competent authority in connection with the submission of Conventions and Recommendations, on the re-examination at appropriate intervals *inter alia* of Recommendations to which effect has not yet been given, and on questions arising out of reports to be made on such texts.

107 Doc. A 37/6, para. 16. The report does not detail the activities in question. According to the press, they have included consumer boycotts of the products of companies considered not to be in full compliance with the Code.

108 For some, such as the Codex Alimentarius standards, the "law of the market place" may constitute sufficient persuasion.

general rules laid down in conventions or recommendations. Many of them represent, perhaps, a service to Member States rather than an expression of the community concerns represented by and in the organization. However that may be, it is necessary, at least as a research function, for international secretariats and expert bodies to have some awareness of the extent to which this type of instrument influences national action.

Procedures for the implementation of resolutions are adopted on an *ad hoc* basis; they are used in some cases and not in others.[109] There have been some resolutions of the United Nations General Assembly in respect of which a follow-up procedure was established by the Assembly[110] and has functioned effectively. The main example is no doubt that of the Declaration on the Granting of Independence to Colonial Countries and Peoples.[111] The Declaration was adopted in 1960. The following year the General Assembly noted with regret that the terms of the Declaration had not yet been implemented and decided to establish a Special Committee to examine the application of the Declaration, to make suggestions and recommendations and to report to the General Assembly.[112] Thereafter the General Assembly gave annual consideration to the report of the Special Committee and brought its authority to bear on particular questions highlighted by the Committee. As regards certain other resolutions, although no special machinery was established, the General Assembly has ensured a regular follow-up on the basis of reports of the Secretary-General and of other organs and subsidiary bodies of the United Nations assigned relevant tasks by the Assembly. Examples are the Declaration on the Strengthening of International Security[113] and the Resolution on Permanent Sovereignty over Natural Resources.[114]

[109] In the absence of specific procedures the terms of particular resolutions may be given weight by reliance on them in other procedures. For instance, in various I.L.O. procedures relating to freedom of association reference has been made to Conference resolutions regarding the independence of the trade union movement (1952) and trade union rights and civil liberties (1970).

[110] The matters dealt with in the Universal Declaration of Human Rights have been regularly reviewed through the machinery of the U.N. Economic and Social Council.

[111] G.A. Res. 1514(XV). [112] G.A. Res. 1654(XVI).

[113] G.A. Res. 2734(XXV). [114] G.A. Res. 1803(XVII).

All the existing Codes of Conduct for multinational enterprises are accompanied by institutional arrangements for monitoring their effectiveness; these arrangements were established either by decision of the competent body of the organization concerned[115] or provided for in the text of the instrument.[116] Analogous provisions are included in the drafts of the two Codes which are still under consideration, the United Nations comprehensive text and the U.N.C.T.A.D. instrument on transfer of technology. An exceptionally wide range of procedures is envisaged in the three existing texts. The I.L.O. and U.N.C.T.A.D. texts provide for reports by governments. All three instruments provide for the establishment of a body concerned with evaluation of information and, more generally, implementation of the texts: the O.E.C.D. Committee on International Investment and Multinational Enterprises (I.M.E. Committee); the I.L.O. (Governing Body) Committee on Multinational Enterprises; and the Intergovernmental Group of Experts on Restrictive Business Practices. The O.E.C.D. and U.N.C.T.A.D. procedures lay some emphasis on intergovernmental consultations to resolve conflicts: thus the O.E.C.D. Council decision provides that Member countries may request that consultations be held in the I.M.E. Committee on any problem arising from the fact that multinational enterprises are made subject to conflicting requirements, and that governments concerned will co-operate with a view to resolving such problems; Section F 4 of the U.N.C.T.A.D. instrument provides for analogous requests and, given its non-binding nature, specifies that States "should accord full consideration" to such requests. The O.E.C.D. and I.L.O. procedures include provision for the "clarification" of the instruments;[117] this is intended, and has proved in practice,[118] to be a

[115] Decision of the O.E.C.D. Council on Inter-Governmental Consultation Procedures on the Guidelines for Multinational Enterprises (C (76) 117, revised in 1979); Decisions of the I.L.O. Governing Body of March 1978 and November 1980.

[116] Sections F and G of the U.N.C.T.A.D. Set of Multilaterally Agreed Equitable Principles and Rules for the Control of Restrictive Business Practices.

[117] The U.N.C.T.A.D. provision giving the Group of Experts, *inter alia*, the power "to make appropriate reports and recommendations to States on ... the application and implementation of the set of Multilaterally Agreed Equitable Principles and Rules" may also cover such clarification.

[118] See, e.g., R. Blanpain, *The Badger Case and the O.E.C.D. Guidelines for Multinational Enterprises* (1977).

form of dispute settlement, not through censure of the conduct of individual governments or companies, but through guidance on the meaning of the texts in the light of particular situations, leaving it to those concerned to draw the appropriate conclusions. Finally, the U.N.C.T.A.D. text makes detailed provision for technical assistance and other advisory or training services.

Non-governmental bodies[119] are given a role in the implementation procedures by O.E.C.D. and I.L.O.; indeed, the former strengthened that role on the occasion of the 1979 review of the Guidelines. In the I.L.O., the participation of employers' and workers' organizations in the regular supervision of the Declaration — reports of governments and their evaluation — is analogous to that given them in respect of international labour Conventions and Recommendations.[120] In O.E.C.D., the I.M.E. Committee is required to invite the Business and Industry and the Trade Union Advisory Committees periodically to express their views and may do so additionally at their request. In O.E.C.D. individual enterprises may state their views on issues concerning the Guidelines which affect their interests;[121] in the I.L.O. the views of enterprises and their staffs are intended to be channelled through employers' and workers' organizations. In the I.L.O., employers' and workers' organizations are expressly empowered to submit certain questions to the I.L.O. for clarification; while this is not specified in O.E.C.D. it corresponds to practice.

The various procedures used for the implementation of non-binding instruments have been described at length because they constitute a means for organizations to promote standards established by their organs amongst all Members, irrespective of their express acceptance.[122] At the same time two problems should be

[119] The U.N.C.T.A.D. text contains substantive provisions addressed to multinational enterprises, but does not envisage non-governmental participation in the implementation procedures.

[120] Seep, 127, note 106.

[121] Individual enterprises were also called upon to signify their acceptance of the Guidelines expressly.

[122] Another, perhaps unique, procedure for promoting the standards of the Organization among the entire membership is the I.L.O. freedom of association complaints procedure, based on the enunciation of the principle of freedom of association in the Constitution of the Organization. The case law developed through that procedure amounts to the establishment of more detailed standards on the subject. See C.W. Jenks, "The International

mentioned. The first is that of the position of minorities opposed to the adoption of the text. It is probably not as serious an issue as might be believed. Apart, possibly, from a small number of resolutions of the General Assembly of the United Nations — which attract excessive attention — there is no evidence of majorities riding roughshod over opposition in the adoption of non-binding standard-setting instruments. Furthermore, the main weapon of implementation procedures — the force of international opinion — derives its strength from the degree of true[123] consensus on the standard to be implemented.

The second problem, of a different nature, is that of the multiplication of procedures and bodies for the implementation of international instruments. To begin with, there were constitutional procedures in certain organizations, bearing on Conventions and Recommendations. Then some Conventions, particularly in the field of human rights, established special machinery for the verification of their application. There is now, increasingly, special machinery also for certain non-binding instruments. As in the case of the multiplicity of legislating bodies, this creates difficulties of coordination of the work of different organs, both within[124] and between organizations, and poses the risk that a growing burden of reports and analysis on governments and international Secretariats will lead to diminishing returns. There is no ready solution because the proliferation of standards and of measures for their implementation is a reflection of the complexity of international relations and activities and of the inability of existing institutions to control them effectively.

D. The Purpose of Standards

Whether standards are in the form of treaties or of non-binding instruments, the concern of organizations is the translation into

Protection of Trade Union Rights", *The International Protection of Human Rights* (D. Evan Luard, ed., 1967), p. 210.

[123] As opposed to procedural consensus under which opposition is expressed by reservations rather than votes.

[124] In the I.L.O., the procedures for the "clarification" of the Tripartite Declaration on Multinational Enterprises may operate only where other procedures (constitutional supervisory machinery or freedom of association complaints) are not applicable.

effect of the responses to a variety of national and international problems which these standards represent. The legal rules and procedures which may be traditionally associated with one or other form of instrument are of value only to the extent that they in fact support that aim. From that point of view, a number of suggestions which have been made in recent years, although in varying degrees shocking to the legal mind, may nevertheless not be devoid of interest.

There have been repeated proposals by developing countries that it should be possible, in ratifying certain conventions in the economic and social fields, to accept their standards only as a goal and to adapt the manner and pace of their detailed implementation to the country's development. Such proposals blur the distinction between conventions with precise requirements, promotional conventions and non-binding instruments. Yet the very existence of the intermediate category — the promotional convention — seems to indicate that such an approach is possible for future instruments and that the real question is what may be gained by it, as compared with a more traditional position which would postpone ratification to the moment when full compliance is possible. The very considerable degree of flexibility already given in special provisions of many conventions, permitting developing countries to attain certain of their standards by stages, implies the judgment that a legal commitment to gradual compliance is useful, particularly where there is effective supervisory machinery. At the same time, the flexibility clauses used at present require a minimum level of immediate obligation. Whether it is either necessary or desirable to go even further in meeting the inability of certain countries to comply with standards at an early date — in particular, whether ratification in such case provides any leverage which periodic review of the application of non-ratified conventions could not provide — is a matter of political judgment.[125]

A less far-reaching variant of such proposals is that designed to permit ratification of conventions on the basis of "substantial equivalence", *i.e.* the achievement of their aims by means different

[125] During the discussion of international labour standards at the 1984 session of the International Labour Conference, many speakers considered that flexibility had to have limits. In particular, it was stressed that "international standards must be intransigent when they are a matter of fundamental rights".

from those expressly laid down. Some recent international labour conventions expressly permit this with respect to certain technical requirements; one such instrument — the Merchant Shipping (Minimum Standards) Convention, 1976 — requires ratifying States to have safety standards, social security measures and conditions of employment substantially equivalent to those laid down in specified earlier Conventions. The problem raised by such proposals and clauses is an essentially practical one, namely that of agreeing on the aims of the express provisions and the extent to which there is indeed equivalence in their achievement.

Converse proposals, from countries which on occasion find compliance with standards easier than the formalities of ratification, have sought means of obtaining formal recognition of the effective application of the terms of conventions even in the absence of legal commitment. Procedures for this purpose were considered and adopted by the International Labour Conference as early as 1947,[126] although they have not been used in practice. Concern then expressed — and no doubt still valid today — was that such procedures might undermine the process of acceptance of legal obligations. This focuses attention on the features of such acceptance which serve to advance the purposes of standards more than effective compliance without obligation. Perhaps the crucial element is that obligation provides some guarantee of continuity of compliance — where and to the extent that the power of denunciation is circumscribed.

[126] Record of Proceedings of the 30th Session of the International Labour Conference, pp. 374-5.

Conclusion

In some ways the position of international organizations in international law is reminiscent of the status of women in national law. It is accepted — with varying degrees of enthusiasm — that they are subjects of the law with a claim to rights and obligations equivalent to those of States, where a need for different treatment is not inherent in their nature. At the same time, there is controversy as to the "inherent" differences and their implications. The imagination to define the needs that are different from those of States and to provide appropriate solutions is signally lacking. Inertia, far more than active resistance, is an obstacle to adaptation of the law even where particular needs are identified.

As in the case of the status of women, a prerequisite of progress would seem to be education, both of those directly concerned within and without the organizations and of those with whom they have to deal. This may be easier said than done. A majority of international organizations — possibly a substantial majority — do not have legal services; sophistication in matters of international law can hardly be expected of their policy-making staff. Even in organizations with legal services many lawyers are likely to be recruited and used for the preparation of contracts, for staff disputes and for issues of internal procedure rather than for problems of international law. Delegates to all but the major political organizations are likely to be technicians to whom such questions are alien. A great and central responsibility lies on the legal services of foreign offices, but how much time and energy have they to devote to these issues and, for that matter, how regularly are they consulted?

A related prerequisite is that of continuity in staffing and in representation. Service in international organizations used to be seen as a career; now the emphasis is on secondment, interchange between jobs inside and outside the organization, and fixed-term contracts. Yet the knowledge and understanding acquired and passed on by career public servants do not find their equivalent in computerized information retrieval systems. As regards delegates, the role which is sometimes played by "elder statesmen" is eloquent testimony to the importance of experience. Very few acquire it as staff move from one government department to another or from a permanent mission to an embassy.

Probably there is also a need for far more contact between like-minded countries, and between groups of such countries, on the types of questions which have been raised here. There is a tendency to see the "group" system as a factor of politicization and hence as nefarious. It can have that effect, particularly on emotive issues. But it is, in a sense, unavoidable, just as the formation of parties has been a natural accompaniment of parliamentary democracy. Groups and parties may have collective knowledge and experience which the individual representative lacks. In the work of the I.L.O., the influence of employers' and workers' representatives is largely due to the fact that they work through cohesive groups, with well-informed secretariats and established procedures for the exchange of views and the elaboration of joint positions. Concertation among governments also is now increasing. However, it has yet to be used for matters of long-range importance; contacts exclusively during the meetings of an organization are not sufficient for that purpose.

Is it then an inescapable conclusion that the law relating to international organizations is not only inadequate but is likely to remain so? There appears to be little ground for optimism. Nevertheless, the mere fact that a number of the questions which have been considered here are now receiving widespread attention holds out some hope. An important test, in the next two or three years, will be the outcome of the consideration of the subject of treaties between States and international organizations, referred to at some length in Chapter I. For the first time systematic consideration is being given to the adaptations necessary in a particular field to make international law applicable to international organizations. If tenable solutions are found both for the outstanding substantive issues and for the procedural problems of associating the organizations with these solutions, this may pave the way for giving, in the long term, full legal recognition to the place international organizations occupy in fact.

Index

Index

For EU product safety concerns, contact us at Calle de José Abascal, 56–1°, 28003 Madrid, Spain or eugpsr@cambridge.org.

www.ingramcontent.com/pod-product-compliance
Lightning Source LLC
Chambersburg PA
CBHW071248180926
51613CB00002B/161
* 9 7 8 1 0 0 9 4 4 8 1 8 5 *